Survive

and

Thrive

in Your

Job Search

THE TEAM NETWORKING GROUP
PROCESS TO YOUR NEXT JOB

Dale Hinshaw, Tom Faulconer, and Mike Johnson

abbott press

Abbott Press books may be ordered through booksellers or by contacting:

Abbott Press
1663 Liberty Drive
Bloomington, IN 47403
www.abbottpress.com
Phone: 1 (866) 697-5310

ISBN: 978-1-4582-2208-4 (sc)
ISBN: 978-1-4582-2207-7 (e)

Library of Congress Control Number: 2018910409

Print information available on the last page.

Abbott Press rev. date: 09/21/2018

CONTENTS

PART 1
How It All Started

PART 2
Learning About Yourself

PART 3
Learning the Tools and Techniques

ACKNOWLEDGEMENTS

Conducting an effective job search is a team effort. Writing a book like this one is no less so. While much of the information has been culled from personal experiences, the authors are very grateful to the many people who offered support, guidance, and content for this project.

Thanks go to...

"Mr. Resume," Don Bauder, and LinkedIn expert and Career Coach, Julie Bondy Roberts, for their knowledge, wisdom, and experience in providing content as well as reviewing relevant portions and providing invaluable feedback.

Professor Ofer Sharone, a friend of Team Networking Group, for his counsel, guidance, support, and research.

Faith Murrell, Grace Murrell, and Ron Brumbarger of Apprentice University and Author Assist for their friendship and, more importantly, their keen eyes, editing, and graphic production skills.

Earle Hart and the Passport to Employment Team for their support and for building an amazing ministry helping those that are unemployed and underemployed to find new careers. What Earle started and his team perpetuates is simply unparalleled.

Team Networking Group members past and present for providing so much of the lessons and, therefore, the content you read in these pages.

Our group of volunteers, all of whom are veterans of the Team Networking group, who helped with choosing a title as well as crafting a marketing plan for this book. Thank you, Diane Kostyshyn, Tony Guisinger, Marty Bird, Lisa Davis, and Tony Brown.

The people who let us ask some uncomfortable questions about their job search journey in order to share them with others, to show it can be done, and to spread a hopeful message. Thanks to Jeff Echols, Tim Maniscalo, Eric Dudley, Matt Belanger, Jim Evans, Pat Dillon, David Gafford, and Lori Harris ... plus a few that elected to remain nameless!

Bruce Flanagan for his insights and for his book, *It's Not About You, It's About Them.*

And all of our families for their love and support.

Dale Hinshaw, Tom Faulconer, Mike Johnson

INTRODUCTION

Imagine for a minute that you are meeting someone new. Perhaps you went to the gym one morning, noticed the person on the treadmill next to you had on a T-shirt with your college crest, and you struck up a conversation. Or maybe you caught someone's eye at the coffee shop, started chatting, and ended up exchanging phone numbers. Whatever the circumstance, you found a strong connection with this new acquaintance and you both agree to talk later and try to get together.

Later in the day, you mention that you met this person to another friend who tells you all the good things he or she has heard about this person and how lucky you are to be connected! You feel excited at the prospect of getting to know this person.

You anxiously finish your daily activities, return home, drop your armload of stuff, fish the person's number from your pocket, and quickly dial it, looking forward to the next step in this budding relationship.

But instead of a warm and inviting voice, you hear a recording that says:

"Thank you for calling. Unfortunately, I get so many phone calls that I cannot answer each one individually. Please leave me a message after the tone. Sometime in the future, a computer program will scan your message to see if anything you have said would interest me. If the scan is positive, I will then listen to your message and determine if I would like to talk with you further. Provided I am interested in talking further, you will receive a phone call from one of my assistants who will spend a few minutes with you verifying that you do, indeed, have something interesting to say. In that case, I will be happy to return your call. This process may take several weeks or even months."

"Because of my busy schedule, you will only hear back from me or one of my assistants if there is actually something interesting in the message you leave."

"Also, please do not visit me, send me a letter, or try to contact me through social networking sites. This phone number is the only way to reach me."

"I thoroughly appreciate your interest in talking to me!"

Huh?

How do you feel about your new friend now? Chances are you wouldn't bother leaving a message and would have a pretty bad taste for your new "friend," right?

Unfortunately, this is exactly the way job seekers are treated in today's environment. Companies spend lots of time and money competing for awards, changing cultures, and advertising their corporate values in an effort to attract good candidates to job opportunities. Then, once a candidate is interested, the candidate is typically treated like so much cattle, completely ignored, made empty promises, and given very little – if any – information during the process.

Depending on the source, reports indicate that people only stay on the job somewhere between 3.6 and 4.6 years. And those ages twenty-five to thirty-four only stay slightly over three years! Companies often lament this fact, complaining that they can't find good people who will stay. Is it any wonder, when companies create an atmosphere in which employment candidates are shown early on that the company only cares about itself? Most people today believe that company loyalty is dead and everyone needs to look out for himself!

That is the climate you are likely to encounter as you launch your job search.

But, before you despair and concede defeat, you should know that you hold the secrets to not only playing this game but to winning it! In this book, you will learn tools and techniques that have been applied hundreds and thousands of times, each one resulting in a new career. For some the process is slow, for some fast. But it is a process and one that is very learnable.

You will find stories from real people that the authors have helped in the past, people from whose experiences and mistakes you can learn. Most important, you will find hope in these pages.

The authors know that God has a plan for you. (As Tom Faulconer says, He must also have a sense of humor to put people through this type of thing!) You will likely not understand this plan while going through the experience, but we can virtually guarantee that someday in the future, you will look back with clarity and say, "Ah! That's why that happened." In the meantime, be patient and trust in yourself, trust in this process, and trust in God.

This book is different than other job search books you will find on the shelf. We didn't write this to tell you how to do it; we wanted to show you. So most chapters will include at least one exercise to reinforce the topic from that section. Please don't skip over these exercises. They are an important part of the self-discovery as well as the job search process. You will find value in them!

Second, the authors' backgrounds are different. Dale Hinshaw brings decades of experience as a Human Resource VP and Director, as well as owner of a staffing company. Dale's most recent decade has been committed to a ministry of helping others find fulfilling employment. This book is the culmination of Dale's tried and true techniques and advice.

Mike Johnson is an accomplished career coach. But that is his second career. He spent many years as a professional with IBM and when he was offered an early retirement package before he was exactly ready to retire, he went through some of the same issues you are likely feeling. What would he do next? What options were open to him? What shape would the "next chapter" in work life take? After much reflection, self-assessment, and some coaching, it was clear that Mike's passion is in helping others in career search and development as well. Mike became a Certified Professional Coach®, and his business, *Coach for Tomorrow*, was born!

Tom Faulconer had a very successful and fulfilling career in the financial services industry. When his tenure as (high-placed and well-compensated) executive at his company came to an end, he immersed himself in the job search. Finding another, comparable, corporate job proved quite difficult and, as he learned more and more about the job search process, he found that people began asking him for help when they became unemployed. Using his background as an attorney, business professor, and Certified Financial Planner®, he started a company helping those in transition, including job transitions, called Transitions Financial LLC.

The three of us each bring a unique perspective to the job search and we have tried very hard to parlay those experiences into a step-by-step guide that will put you back to work in the best job with the best company in the shortest time.

You deserve to be happy and successful.

A fulfilling career is just around the corner!

PART 1
HOW IT ALL STARTED

CHAPTER ONE
The Dale Hinshaw Story

Over the past few weeks, a job seeker who is part of my Team Networking Group has been working hard on landing a new position with a company that, while outside of his past industry, would be a very nice fit. He just needs to convince the hiring company of that fact. To that end, Jim has been networking with others in this new industry to learn as much as he can so he can "talk the talk" during his interviews. One of Jim's best networking connections has been a high-placed person at a similar company in another city.

Jim's connection has spent his entire career in this industry; he's well-known, well-liked, and well-respected. He is the entire package, as they say. He has been invaluable to Jim, lending him insight and guiding him through the application and interview process. He's even been most generous in sharing his connections inside Jim's target company.

This morning, Jim's connection was let go.

This story may sound very familiar to you. It may have happened to you recently. It may have happened to you in the past. It may well have happened to you multiple times.

Frankly, there is an epidemic in the United States affecting mostly middle-aged workers (although losing one's job is in no way confined to that age group) who are finding themselves suddenly and unexpectedly out of a job they have held for years and proved successful in time and time again. Many of these people never considered working anywhere else and diligently looked toward a nice retirement party and a hardy send-off.

Now, that isn't going to happen.

My Team Networking Group, which I will explain in much greater detail in the coming chapters, caters to those individuals. Virtually every week, one or more new unemployed people will show up at our weekly meetings, distraught, surprised, and anxious. In my old military days, we called it "shell shock." They want to know what to do and how to do it. They harbor secret hopes that the company which let them go will suddenly realize the error of its ways and beg them to return. They fear the stigma that often comes with being out of work.

They also have questions. "How do I go about finding another job?" I commonly hear people ask, "I haven't looked for a job in twenty years! What do I do first?" But by far, the question that I receive the most is also the one I have no answer for: "How long will it take to find another job?"

If you have picked up this book, you are most likely either someone currently "in transition" – the buzzword for someone out of work--and anxious to find the answers to those and other questions for yourself, or you are in a job that helps people find their next job. You may be a human resource professional, career coach, or you may work with an outplacement firm.

Frankly, there is an epidemic in the United States affecting mostly middle-aged workers who are finding themselves suddenly and unexpectedly out of a job they had held for years and proved successful in time and time again.

Regardless, the following pages will help you. If you are a job seeker, I can't tell you when you will find your next job. I can tell you that the tools and techniques, the data and stories, the successes and failures contained in this book, will give you the blueprint you need to successfully conduct your job search. And even though you will experience times of doubt (interspersed with times of euphoria and optimism), I can tell you that the process will work. Trust the process, trust God, and you will be successful. I guarantee that.

My name is Dale Hinshaw. I have devoted my entire (and long) career to helping people find jobs that they are passionate about. After serving in the military, I chose human resources as my profession. (Confidentially, I am old enough that it was called "personnel" back then!). I have served in a Human Resources Vice President role for a couple of different companies. I have also owned a staffing agency. Currently, I devote my time and effort to helping people in transition with practical guidance on finding a job, networking, job search skills, and, most importantly, spiritual guidance and support.

Being out of work is one of the most difficult, depressing, and deflating experiences anyone goes through. But know that you have in your hands your roadmap to success, in addition to the friends, family, and even strangers out there just waiting to help you. You will be okay.

After spending as many years as I have in the human resources space, I would like to start this book by claiming I know everything there is to know about finding a job. I'd like to tell you that, but I can't. I am smart enough, however, to know many people who are experts in their own rights that have helped put this manual together for your benefit. From Dr. Ofer Sharone, a Harvard trained lawyer-turned international unemployment expert, to Don Bauder, one of the best resume writers in the business, to Julie Bondy Roberts, a producer of "badass" LinkedIn profiles, to hundreds of TNG alumni, this book will bring you the best and most current information from some of the most knowledgeable sources available.

If you have lots of free time (which happens sometimes to people in between jobs), Google job search books. You will get page after page of results. So, a logical question would be, why am I writing another one?

Don't get me wrong, there are some very good books out there on job searching. There are also many that are little more than gimmicks. You will see titles that promise you can find your dream job in three days, tell you that you only have to work on your search for five minutes a day, or claim that no one needs resumes anymore. We all like to think we are learning the secret way to do something, and titles and promises like those are sure to tempt the most desperate of job seekers. "Wait! You mean everyone else is really doing it wrong but you are going to tell me the magic formula? And for only $34.99?"

You can probably guess that there is no real magic formula. Do some people actually find a job in five minutes a day? Is there anyone out there that landed their next great gig in three days? Sure. But they are the exception, not the rule. The right approach is to work hard utilizing the tools and techniques that are proven to work again and again. And if someone hires you in three days, count your blessings and get back to work! But counting on finding something by some rogue design and *not* doing the tried and true things is a dangerous path to take.

This book is based, first, on my experiences as a career coach and human resources professional. I will be sharing the things that have worked for hundreds of my clients and group members as well as the insights of the experts I mentioned above. There is a game plan for your job search in these pages. And that game plan is backed up, not only by the success of others, but by scientific research that provides proof that what you are about to start on is the shortest road to a new job.

The right approach is to work hard utilizing the tools and techniques that are proven time and time again to work.

If you aren't already, in the coming weeks you will often be overwhelmed with feelings of despair and even jealousy as others find success before you. It's okay to feel that way. Just remind yourself to be happy for them because your time is coming! You will find yourself questioning your past successes and wondering to yourself – or maybe even aloud – if you really have any value for an employer. Those questions are natural for people to ask when they are out of work, especially when the decision to leave the last job was not their own.

But here's some important information: there's nothing wrong with you. There's plenty wrong with the system used to find employment and there's not much we can do about that except play the game as it is. Not hearing back or getting a rejection for a job you are perfect for is not about you. It's about the system.

You will likely think you must have done something really wrong in your life to deserve what you are going through. But here's the thing: life is very similar to a jigsaw puzzle. You can't tell what the finished product will look like until virtually all the pieces are in place. If you knew that you were going to be out of work for three months, then land a job that is a level higher and pays more than your previous position, you'd gladly go through this process. If you knew that you were going to be able to spend time with an elderly relative while you are off – something you never would have had time to do while working – you would probably be okay with your hiatus. I am a firm believer that things happen for a reason, and your situation is no different. The problem is, like the jigsaw puzzle, you won't know the reason until later. Only then will it make sense.

Trust the system. Trust God. You are an awesome person and an asset that your next company needs and is looking for.

Good luck in your search!

Now, let's get started finding your next great job ...

CHAPTER TWO

The Team Networking Group Way

In 2009, after working with several different job search support organizations in my area, I embarked on a new idea. I rented a room at a local church and began hosting a networking group for job seekers, mostly higher-level executives who found themselves out of work due to the recent market crash. Many of these extremely accomplished individuals had never needed to look for work before and never dreamed they would be asked to leave their current positions. Some had severance packages to help them survive, but most did not.

As Team Networking Group, or TNG, progressed over the next several years, it achieved a reputation for being a safe place for displaced executives to network with others in the same situation, to gain support and focus, and to bring structure and accountability to their job search activities.

During this same time, the meetings have taken on a loose but effective structure. Each meeting begins at 9:00 in the morning, with each participant giving a brief introduction of himself (for many, this is a good time to develop and practice their thirty second "elevator" speech) to succinctly say what each person is looking for and to update the group on activities from the past week. Such activities include people that each person networked with, jobs applied for, and companies targeted.

These introductions usually last an hour. This is followed by a presenter whom I have secured in the local community. The presenters range from career coaches to recruiters, HR professionals to experts on social media. Eventually, as the group has been successful in helping people find jobs, I have asked alumni to return and share their stories.

We typically wrap up the morning with some sort of job search practice, perhaps reciting and critiquing each other's STAR stories (you'll learn what those are in another chapter), or even holding mock interviews within the group to help a member prepare for an actual upcoming interview.

To date, our support efforts have assisted over 650 people into their next career. These successes include a retired major general in the U.S. Army, three college professors, a pharmacist, a company president, numerous company vice presidents, CIOs, CFOs, and others.

It became clear to me that whatever we were doing at TNG was working better than anything else we had tried in the past. But, frankly, I didn't really know why.

The TNG platform has given members reasons to connect with and get to know many, many people with whom they might not otherwise have crossed paths. One of those is an assistant professor at the Massachusetts Institute of Technology named Ofer Sharone. Professor Sharone's research focuses on career transitions and unemployment. In 2013, he authored *Flawed System/Flawed Self: Job Searching and Unemployment Experiences*. He is highly accomplished, holding a law degree from Harvard and a Ph.D. in Sociology from the University of California, Berkeley.

The TNG platform has given members reasons to connect with and get to know many, many people with whom they might not otherwise have crossed paths.

Given our parallel interests, Professor Sharone and I began to collaborate on some projects and surveys together. When I emailed the professor and told him of my idea for this book, he was encouraging and kind enough to send me some research with which he was familiar. He also alerted me to his own research in his book.

The culmination of the research, involving dozens of scientific and academic studies, was a 2014 research paper by Songqi Liu of Pennsylvania State University, Jason L. Huang of Wayne State University, and Mo Wang of the University of Florida. This research paper, unknowingly and independently, scientifically explains the success of TNG.

Most job seekers assume that the job search process is a solitary and lonely endeavor. And for many, whether by choice or by ignorance of alternatives, it certainly is. It is taxing mentally, physically, and emotionally, takes a toll on families, stretches and even ruins financial plans, and increases the likelihood of depression. But people involved in what the study authors call a "job search intervention" are much more likely to find a job quicker, survive physically and mentally, be financially stronger, and avoid experiencing depression.

The authors of the study define a job search intervention as "any type of training program designed to help job seekers look for employment or secure employment faster." Given this broad definition, many different programs and opportunities for job seekers fall under this umbrella.

Amazingly, I discovered that TNG has borne out all the facts in this scientific research over and over again, as the group has been offering virtually all of the different job search interventions (and much more) explained in the research paper.

The Likelihood of Getting a Job

The most common question newly unemployed job seekers ask is how long the process will take. That is also the one question that no one can answer with any authority. The U.S. Bureau of Labor Statistics publishes numbers on occasion providing the average time the average person is unemployed. I suppose I could even calculate the numbers from my experience with TNG and other groups. But the problem with such a methodology is that no one is average.

A TNG member who was one of our longer-term job seekers offered this revelation: "I think finding a job is like a gumball machine when you were little. You wanted the big purple jawbreaker and you might put quarter after quarter in the machine and not get that jawbreaker. You may watch some other kid drop a quarter in and get it on his first try and wonder why that didn't happen for you. It's even conceivable that the purple jawbreaker may be the very last one to be dispensed. No one can tell you when your gumball is coming."

We have had plenty of people come to a single TNG meeting and return the next week with news of a new job (not necessarily as a result of the TNG experience but still celebrated with the required donuts!). We've had very sharp, very qualified people who remain in the group for months or even years. No one can say when the gumball is coming.

However, based on the extensive research conducted by the authors of the study, we can say that the likelihood – or, if you prefer, the odds – of your landing a job, increase depending on the effective activities that you engage in. In fact, those that participated in the type of job search interventions that we offer at TNG were 2.67 times more likely to find a job than those who approached the process without help.

> **The likelihood of your landing a job increases depending on the effective activities that you engage in.**

That encouraging statistic might be interpreted two different ways. First, a person is 2.67 times more likely to get a job this month due to her involvement in some sort of formal job search program (the "intervention"). Or, the time it takes to find a job is 2.67 times longer for those that go it alone.

Either way, the result is staggering!

Because there are so many components of a job search and so many different types of interventions available to job seekers, it is quite helpful to break these down even further and attempt to identify which are the most effective to employ in the search. Luckily, the researchers did this as well.

Teaching Job Search Skills

The job search process has significantly changed in the last twenty or twenty-five years. The advent of technology has antiquated the days of circling ads in the newspaper, cold-calling companies, and showing up asking to complete an application. Today's job skills include things like resume optimization, All-Star LinkedIn profiles, effective social media use, enrollment in online courses, and finding the right job search websites for your career and level. At TNG, we have weekly speakers who help our job seekers in each of these skills and more.

The research indicates that helping a person with these job search skills, as opposed to allowing him to discover them and how to use them on his own, increases the likelihood that he will find a job by 3.32 times!

At this point, you may be somewhat confused. By incorporating a job search intervention technique, a person is 2.67 times more likely to get a job. But at the same time, learning job search skills increases it by 3.32 times. Both are true. The likelihood of finding a job using ANY job search intervention technique at all – any of the several tested in the study – will increase your success rate by 2.67 times. Learning and implementing these specific job search skills will do even more, increasing your odds by 3.32 times.

Improving Your Self-Presentation

Your self-presentation is, in effect, your brand. Social workers define it as the attempt to control images of yourself before an audience.[1]

---

[1] Schlenker, Barry R. and Leary, Mark R, "Social Anxiety and Self-Presentation: A Conceptualization and Model," *Psychological Bulletin*, Vol. 92, No 3, 641-669, Print.

Promoting yourself, whether on paper through your marketing materials, or by phone during a screening interview, or in person when interviewing with a company, is an important factor in the job search. People often make snap judgments about others in the first few seconds of meeting them. A weak handshake, no eye contact, or sitting uncomfortably in the interview chair can all cost a well-qualified candidate the job.

While no one particularly likes criticism, at TNG we have discovered that holding mock interviews, encouraging members to make presentations on relevant topics, and asking for reactions – good and bad – from the other members, is an incredibly valuable exercise.

The research supports this method. Increasing one's self-promotion skills increases the job seeker's likelihood of getting a job by 3.4 times. Put another way, you are 340% more likely to get a job if you work on your self-promotion skills!

The Importance of Self-Confidence

There's an old saying that the only time a bank will loan you money is when you don't need it. If you're broke, they won't give you any! The same is true in the job search. Job seekers are often at their lowest point emotionally, filled with self-doubt, and even battling depression. Yet they are expected to be "on" whenever going in for an interview. Most people are not their most confident selves when they are out of work. And most employers don't want you if you lack confidence! Research, though, indicates that a job search intervention involving activities that boost a person's self-confidence results in a 340% increase in the likelihood of success in the job search process.

Psychologists have a concept called self-efficacy. Self-efficacy is defined as an individual's belief in his or her capacity to execute behaviors necessary to produce specific performance attainments. In everyday language, that means confidence in one's own motivation and behavior.[2]

TNG does not have presenters on building confidence. However, it provides such support by its very existence. Those who attend the weekly meetings interact with others, make new connections, learn of opportunities, and even schedule informational meetings on the spot. Compared to those job seekers who sit at home day after day trolling online job sites and hoping to hear back, how could this activity not increase a person's confidence? Plus, by participating in the mock interviews and presentation opportunities, members gain further confidence in their abilities.

Proactivity

Proactivity can be explained in terms of what many people hire career coaches to do for them. Proactivity is the encouragement of a job seeker to widen the types of positions considered, to identify transferable skills to open new potential career paths, even to begin applying for positions that perhaps are above the job seeker's current abilities. It also includes actively scheduling informational interviews, meeting people with whom the job seeker is presently unacquainted, following up with companies after applications and interviews, providing unsolicited information to companies after an interview, and asking employers who do not have an appropriate opening if they might know of another company that would.

These activities are quite often outside the comfort zone of job seekers. It feels like you may be intruding, being a pest, and making a nuisance of yourself. Who would hire a pest?

Here is the key to being proactive that virtually all job seekers struggle with: if they like you, following up is not going to change their mind. Likewise, if they don't like you, following up is not going

[2] Carey, Michael P. and Forsyth, Andrew D, "Teaching Tip Sheet: Self Efficacy," http://www.easybib.com/guides/citation-guides/mla-format/how-to-cite-a-website-mla/, Publication Date Unknown, Web, November 17, 2017.

to change their mind. Once again, that position is supported by the test data. Job seekers who were proactive in their activities, compared to those who were not, were 5.88 times more likely to land a job! Of all the methods examined, this one is critical.

A TNG client, Mark, targeted a specific company that he wanted to work for. He made a contact inside the company and provided monthly updates to the insider for a year. Due to Mark's persistence, the hiring manager contacted him and told him that, "When he had a job opening, Mark would be his major candidate." Mark was hired – without any competition!

Goal Setting

Goal setting is important for success in a job and even more important when looking for a job. It is crucial that job seekers have goals for the number of informational meetings to be held each week, the number of new contacts made, even the number of business cards handed out.

Those in the job search mode, especially when their unemployment was unexpected, often feel lackluster. They will find excuses to not do the things to further the job search. Walking the dog and cutting the yard become substitutes for meaningful job search activities. By establishing goals, a job seeker has some accountability. And, when they meet those goals, job seekers feel more accomplished and positive.

It turns out that goal setting is vitally important in the job search. The individuals who set goals were 4.67 times more likely to find a job.

Social Support

Believe it or not, job seekers often find themselves lacking support during the process. And as the process lingers on, what support they may have tends to wane.

Friends and family members, especially those who have not experienced a job search, often do not understand the process. They will offer advice that they believe is helpful but has generally already been tried or is outdated. ("Just go visit some companies and apply!"). You will often have others recommend that you talk to companies by which you were rejected months ago. And, eventually, people may start wondering what is wrong with you since you can't find a job!

One of the consistent issues we deal with at TNG is the lack of support from spouses and sometimes children. We have even had members who won't tell their family they lost their job, instead leaving the house each morning and spending the day at the library or coffee shop. Spouses may raise financial concerns, be worried about having to move and uproot the family, and even be anxious about losing their identity as the spouse of a vice president or director. None of that talk benefits a job seeker.

In addition, it is very common for family members to view a job seeker's attendance at networking events and informational meetings as a waste of valuable time. "You should be out looking for a job, not going to meetings!" Yet networking and informational meetings are exactly what a job seeker should be doing.

A group like TNG offers support. Friendships are made and nurtured. Many people make lifelong connections. No one is going to criticize or bad-mouth another when they are both in the same position.

A group like TNG offers support. Friendships are made and nurtured there. Many people make lifelong connections in our group. No one is going to criticize or bad-mouth another when they are both in the same position.

Those that have emotional support from others--family, friends, or a networking group like TNG--increase their likelihood of job search success by 4.26, or 426%, compared to those with no support system.

The Combination of Job Search-Related Skills and Motivation

Finally, the authors of the research paper tested the efficacy of a job search intervention that provided either job search-related skills or motivation to participants. In this case, job search-related skills included skill development such as identifying job leads, preparing resumes, and mock interviews. Motivation focused on goal setting and self-accountability.

While each of these independently increased the job seeker's likelihood of success, as shown above, the researchers found that a program combining both of these further increased the likelihood of success in finding a job by 3.37 times!

The combination of job search skills and motivation is, truly, the framework upon which the TNG group is built. Our speakers provide regular job search skills training, while the group provides motivation through accountability and social support.

But the TNG success story is told well beyond the scientific research. Over the years, it has become very clear that the TNG model provides other extremely valuable benefits.

Networking

As many as 85% or more of jobs are found through networking. And while using a person's LinkedIn network and having regular and consistent informational meetings is key, a job search group like TNG expands a job seeker's network exponentially.

When opening our weekly sessions, each participant tells a bit about himself, followed by an activity update. During this time, the participant is encouraged to mention any informational meetings and companies he is interested in or has applied to. It is not uncommon that at least one other person in the group has one good, solid contact at the targeted company. And, since all the participants are in the same position of job searching, they are eager and willing to make introductions.

Matt was a high-flyer with IBM. He was on his way up as he approached his 40th birthday and things seemed well-settled for him. He was married, had two young children, and had advanced to the point at IBM where he was eligible for stock options. He liked the Raleigh, NC, area where he lived, although neither his family nor his wife's were nearby.

One day, Matt was contacted by a recruiter about a position in Indianapolis, IN, with an energy company. The job sounded like a dream. The company was interested in making some major changes to its IT infrastructure and that was Matt's specialty. Matt's in-laws were located in Indianapolis and it all sounded too good to pass up. When the energy company offered him the job, he and his family were thrilled.

Moving from Raleigh to Indianapolis with two young kids was no small feat. But the family found their new home welcoming and the kids quickly joined activities in the Indianapolis area that they enjoyed. Even the transition to new schools went smoothly.

After only about six months, the energy company decided that they really didn't need to update their IT infrastructure after all and eliminated Matt's position.

Matt had no real network in the Indianapolis area. He didn't even have enough connections to start scheduling informational meetings.

A friend recommended Matt attend the TNG meetings. As a result, Matt was immediately referred by other members to people he could use to begin building his local network. Within a couple months, Matt was holding several informational meetings each week and became involved in a couple of very high-level IT networking groups, getting to know several CIOs in the area. This level of networking would have taken Matt much, much longer on his own.

Having Lots of People Looking for Your Job

A second critical advantage to the job search group concept is that you are no longer the only one looking for your next job. At any given time, TNG has fifteen to twenty members, each of whom is conducting his own job search, networking, and checking job boards for openings. Although we have no requirement to do so, most attendees take detailed notes as each person gives his activity update. As they come across opportunities in their own searches, they willingly pass them along to others. Some opportunities have wide enough appeal that we distribute them to all attendees via email.

More often, one member will email job leads to another. Most TNG participants receive at least one or two job leads from other members every week! Furthermore, it isn't uncommon that the member passing along the job lead also passes along a connection in the company with an offer to make an introduction.

You might wonder why one job seeker would pass a job lead to another. Of course, the majority of people in the group do not share the same career. So it makes sense that someone in commercial printing would pass along a lead for a medical sales position. But the camaraderie of the group is so strong that often, for example, a marketing director will apply for a position, then pass along the information to another person pursuing a marketing director position. Each member truly looks out for everyone else's best interests.

Accountability

TNG is often referred to as an "accountability" group. Accountability groups are good for job seekers, but TNG has become much more.

In a typical accountability group, each participant is, in effect, beholden to the others to meet certain goals set at each meeting. For example, if Sharon tells the group she plans to hold six informational meetings over the next week, the group expects her to meet that goal and to report on those meetings at the next gathering.

TNG doesn't typically require such outward goal setting, although some participants do announce their plans as a way of holding their own feet to the fire. But even without stated goals, no one likes coming to TNG meetings with nothing to report. A person with no activity is only hurting her own job search chances, but there is an inherent "guilt" factor when everyone announces their activity and one member has nothing to report. Indeed, the normal response of other members is to begin trying to make connections for the person so she can start getting some informational meetings on her calendar. Again, the group truly watches out for each other.

Structure

I have heard plenty of stories about people who lost their job and sat on the couch day after day. Going from a highly structured existence of a nine to five job to literally having nothing to wake up for in the morning is difficult for most job seekers.

Our TNG chapter meets every Wednesday morning from 9 am to noon. It is like a weekly staff meeting. Participants know that this is a set time on their calendars. Even having this one fixed item on the weekly schedule is quite helpful in giving much needed structure to job seekers.

Support

Above all, TNG is a support group. Here is part of the reason why.

Several years ago, a gentleman was referred to TNG. He had lost his job and began attending, applying the things he learned and, in general, was job searching. Unfortunately, as happens occasionally, nothing seemed to be paying off, and he became more and more frustrated.

He related that his wife was less than supportive and simply didn't understand why he hadn't found another job. Unbeknownst to the group, he had moved out of his house to live in his car. His attendance at TNG became sporadic as well. This happens sometimes and, frankly, I didn't think too much of it.

A few weeks later, I received word that the gentleman had taken his own life out of frustration.

At that point, I committed myself to ensure nothing like that would ever happen again. We had let this man down.

Since that happened, I have taken three concrete steps in response. First, I am extremely sensitive to the members of the group. I watch their demeanors, attitudes, etc., and try to be in contact with each of them outside the formality of the TNG meeting. It may simply be a conversation during a break, but I am always on the lookout for signs of despair and danger.

Above all TNG is a support group.

Second, I relate that story to the TNG group every few months (as the group turns over members frequently). I have no doubt that this story is one catalyst in making the group cohesive, and one reason everyone watches out for the others.

Third, we have made lay ministers available to our participants through our host church. Our church operates a very robust program involving trained lay ministers who have wholeheartedly embraced the plight of the job seekers in our group.

Throughout this book, I will be explaining concepts that will help you find your next job as quickly as possible, the Team Networking Group Way!

Exercise:

In this book you will learn many different techniques to help in your job search. The following worksheet should be used to help track your progress in both learning and applying these skills and methods.

Make this sheet your roadmap to job search success!

Job Search Accountability Checklist

Checklist Items	Description	MON	TUE	WED	THR	FRI	SAT	SUN
Basic Information								
Update Resume & Cover Letter								
Resume Reviewed by Others								
Business Cards (2-sided preferred)								
1-page Marketing Statement								
30 Second Introduction								
12 Star Stories Prepared								
T-Letter and Personal Marketing Statement								
Job search Skills Resources and Workshops								
LinkedIn								
Update LinkedIn Profile								
Use LinkedIn for Network & Job Search								
LinkedIn Profile Reviewed								
Attend LinkedIn Training Class								
Contact Info at Top of Profile								
Career Summary – Who You Are								
List Education, Endorsements, & Recommendations								
Networking Meetings								
Research Job Search Support Groups								
Attend Job Search Support Group								
Networking Meetings								
Attend Business/Professional Groups								
Attend Career Fairs								
Informational Meetings								
Phone Calls/Emails								
Informational Interviews								
Email to Set Appointment								
Call to Schedule Interview								
# of Connections Made								

Interview Process									
Submit Applications									
Research for Cover Letter									
Research for Interview									
Phone Call/Visits									
In-Person/Phone Interviews									
2nd Interview or More									
Thank You Notes Sent									
Research Connections/Interviewers									
Improving Skills									
Hours Improving Skills/Education									
Hours Volunteering									
Some Consulting									
Others									

PART 2

LEARNING ABOUT YOURSELF

TNG Strategy: Learn About Yourself, Your Skills and Hidden Talents to Discover What Amazing Things You Offer to Employers

CHAPTER THREE

How Did You Find Yourself in This Position?

N o doubt, if you recently lost your job, you have asked yourself how it happened. After all, you probably did everything you could to avoid this exact scenario. You may have earned a college degree, maybe even two. You were hired by a stable, top-notch company. You did good work and earned regular promotions and raises. And suddenly, you find yourself job-hunting.

In a pre-election debate with then-President Jimmy Carter, Ronald Reagan famously said, "Recession is when your neighbor loses his job. Depression is when you lose yours." In the same vein, chances are your neighbors have been losing their jobs but, since it didn't affect you directly, you didn't think too much about it. But now it's your turn.

My friend Professor Ofer Sharone of MIT, who studies the unemployment process and its effects on people – especially middle-aged, white collar workers -- wrote a book that helps explain this fairly recent phenomenon.

"Over the past thirty years, white-collar employment relations in the United States have been transformed from secure and stable to contingent and precarious ... While blue-collar workers were typically

> *subject to layoffs during economic downturns, white-collar workers,*
> *particularly at large companies, were implicitly promised lifetime*
> *employment and were rarely laid off, even during hard economic times.*
> *For white-collar workers, the firm was often understood as a large*
> *family with long-term attachments and a web of mutual obligations ...*
> *The worker invested in the firm, and the firm invested in the worker."*
> *Flawed System, Flawed Self, Ofer Sharone, p. 5.*

However, since the 1970s, Sharone writes, the job-loss rate has increased more for college-educated white-collar workers than for blue-collar workers or workers who never graduated from college. Consider the import of that statement: a college degree that used to guarantee success now statistically puts you at more risk of job loss than not having one!

Unfortunately, the bad news doesn't stop there. In 2003, the group impacted the most by long-term job loss (defined as twenty-seven weeks or more) was clearly the college educated. Put another way, of those unemployed, workers with a high school education (or less) had an 18% chance of becoming long-term unemployed, while those with some college education were slightly higher, at about 19%. College educated workers had a 23% chance – roughly one in four – of being out of work for at least 27 weeks.[3]

The point of sharing this rather depressing information is definitely not to discourage you. The point is that you are not alone. The best and brightest in every industry have found themselves in the same situation as you are in now. Plus, the good news is, because others have increasingly been subject to this unwanted sabbatical, they have paved the way for you. You can use what they learned in their job searches to find your next job that much easier and faster.

Before we delve into the tools and techniques of the successful job search, let's spend a minute looking at some of the misinformation regarding employment and jobs.

---

[3] Sharone, Ofer, "Introduction," *Flawed System Flawed Self*, 2014, The University of Chicago Press, p. 8

At the time I am writing, the unemployment rate in the United States is reported to be 4.2% of those sixteen years of age and older. That is the lowest in years. In fact, at this same time in 2010 the rate was 9.5%. Reading information like that may understandably make you wonder what is wrong with you. Everyone else seems to be employed but you aren't. But those numbers are very misleading.

The Bureau of Labor Statistics calculates and publishes the monthly unemployment rate but media outlets report it with little to no further explanation. In truth, the unemployment rate is not the rate of unemployment in the country. It is really the percentage of people compared to the entire population of adults sixteen and over who are currently filing claims and/or receiving unemployment benefits. This means that someone who is unemployed and living off his or her savings for a few weeks while looking for a new position is not included in that number. It also means that people who are fortunate enough to not have to file for unemployment benefits are not counted. But the real kicker is that the number also doesn't include those people who have exhausted their unemployment benefits. Given that the definition of long-term unemployment is twenty-seven weeks and the maximum unemployment benefit period is twenty-six weeks, this number excludes many long-term unemployed.

There is no way to know for certain exactly how many or what percentage of people are out of work. That number is just not calculated and reported by the United States government. But there is another rarely reported number that can offer some insight: the labor participation rate.

The labor participation rate is a measure of the active portion of the economy's labor force. It includes the percentage of both the people working and those actively looking for work. Those that have given up and no longer bother looking for a job are not counted in the labor participation rate.

You are not alone and the best and brightest in every industry have found themselves in the same situation as you are now.

In the last ten years, the labor participation rate has steadily dropped, meaning that more and more people are simply leaving the workforce. (I doubt that there are that many lottery winners, and new retirees only make a small dent.) The reality is that people have just quit looking as they face rejection and discouragement at every turn.

Between 1985 and 2009, the labor participation rate remained between 66% and 67% of the eligible workforce. Since 2009, it has been in a statistical freefall. In October 2015, the Bureau of Labor Statistics reported that the rate had hit its lowest point in decades at 62.5%. Since then it has barely recovered, hovering in the high 62% range, occasionally flirting with a very low 63% number.

For the record, that means that the number of people who are not working right now is about 96 million, which seems like an incredibly high number. However, this includes those who are retired, sick, disabled, voluntarily not working (like stay-at-home parents), and students. Still, according to Forbes, this leaves about 5 ½ million people who want to work but don't have a job. Assuming there are around 150,000,000 people who are either in the workforce or looking for work, this means that every 1% decline in the labor participation rate is equal to about 1,500,000 people. So a drop from 66% to 63% indicates that 4,500,000 more people are out of the workforce now than ever before.

Indeed, more and more, the mantra of the middle-aged worker is this: there are two types of workers, the ones who have lost their job and the ones who will.

You, my friend, are in excellent company, and those that have gone before you have done you the favor of making the mistakes and paving the path for your job search journey. Believe me, it will be a journey with twists and turns, hills and valleys. But you will reach your destination (wherever that may be). So buckle your seat belt, adjust your mirrors, and get ready for the ride of a lifetime. Godspeed!

CHAPTER FOUR

Welcome to The Unexpected

For many, it wasn't supposed to be this way.

If you are like most older workers, you probably envisioned yourself working at the same company for many more years. In all the time you have devoted to your organization, you can point to concrete accomplishments that left your mark on the company. What about that system implementation you brought in on time and on budget? Did they just forget about that? How about the new customer you landed that earned you the President's Award? Wasn't that good enough?

For many workers – older and younger – the thought of a job search comes as a big surprise. After all, you may have even been in demand! Headhunters called regularly, trying to lure you away, but you stayed put. Look what it got you, right?

Although it certainly may not make the decisions at your company understandable and certainly not welcome, you may find some comfort in the fact that you are not alone in facing both this life event and the feelings that come with it.

Jeff Echols was at the top of his game. Armed with a degree in architecture, Jeff spent over ten years with a successful architecture firm, eventually developing a specialty in construction management. Soon, others noticed his success.

In the mid-2000s, Jeff was recruited by a pair of architects who owned a firm that wanted to get into the lucrative construction management area. The firm felt that Jeff could help them do just that. After some deliberation, Jeff signed on to handle both construction management and business development, another area in which he excelled.

The construction management division did well, providing new income and substantially higher margins than the traditional architecture projects. Unfortunately, the same couldn't be said of the economy as the crash of 2008-2009 took its toll on many businesses, architecture in particular. With little new building and renovating, drastic measures had to be taken. The two partners called a meeting and announced that everyone, including Jeff, would be taking a 25% pay cut.

Even with the pay cut, Jeff sensed that the firm was in trouble. The partners were just not seeing things eye-to-eye and he feared an impending split. Family and friends told him to find another job before something happened. While a good idea in theory, in practice it was nearly impossible, as unemployment rates among architects approached 40%! There were simply no other jobs around for Jeff.

The eventual partner split soon happened, and Jeff was offered a choice. He could go with partner #1, who was going to continue the business. Or he could go with partner #2, who would be taking the physical assets of the old firm and starting a new firm from scratch, along with a couple other new partners. Jeff took the offer from partner #2, once again to build the construction management and business development for the new venture.

Two short years later, the Indiana Chapter of the American Institute of Architects (AIA) named Jeff's new firm the Firm of the Year in architecture.

Things were going well, to say the least.

Fast forward another two years and on a Friday, Jeff was in Fort Wayne, Indiana, at the AIA regional convention accepting more awards. The firm had, again, been selected as an award winner in architecture and, this time, also received the award for construction management. The firm – and Jeff – were on a roll! Before leaving the convention, Jeff also made a presentation to 150 other architects on marketing themselves.

The following week, Jeff took his family on a well-deserved vacation to Florida. Standing in the airport waiting on a rental car, he received a text message from one of the partners. "We need to talk when you get back." Jeff responded, "Call me now." But the partner declined, simply telling Jeff to enjoy his vacation.

A week later, things were going normally back in the office. Jeff had conducted site visits that morning and held a conference call with a large client. Nothing further had been said about "talking," but Jeff and his employers had a standing 1:30 Monday meeting scheduled. When the partners moved it off site, Jeff thought that strange.

At 1:30, in a small coffee shop, Jeff was told his job was eliminated. He was completely shocked.

The firm had weathered the economic downturn, was growing, being recognized by its peers, and turning a profit. And, frankly, quite a bit of that was due to Jeff's efforts.

For the first time in twenty years, Jeff was out of work. He had no severance, no retirement to fall back on. It was as if someone had flipped a switch on his career from "on" to "off."

Later, Jeff discovered that the firm was preparing a large bid for a state contract. The state expressed concern over the small size of the firm and its ability to perform, so the partners made a decision to cut off the construction management area and reallocate the money (and people) to architecture to help win the big contract.

Jeff had lost his job through no fault of his own.

Many lessons can be learned from Jeff's experience. Let's take a look at a few.

1. *Often times, doing the right thing for you and for the business will not guarantee recognition of your successes.*

Many jobs in companies become microcosms of political positions. There isn't a politician in office who is liked by everyone. And the higher up the office, the more people take sides for and against that person. National officeholders often win elections by very narrow margins. Indeed, the largest victory by a United States President in the popular vote was just 61.05% for Lyndon Johnson in 1964. On top of that, only 62.8% of people even voted. So, arguably, the most popular president at the time of election was disliked by more than half of the country!

2. *Second-guessers are rampant in business!*

The majority of people who leave their job cite their boss as the main reason. One survey by Gallup Research in 2015 reported that only 18% of managers possessed a "high degree" for managing talent. Shockingly, that survey was not of employees but of the managers themselves! The survey further posits that only 35% of managers are actively engaged in their work and workplaces. Over half – 51% -- reported not being engaged, and the remaining 14% reported active disengagement![4]

If that startling information is indeed accurate, the chances are very good that you have worked for a manager that just doesn't care if you do a good job! Proving yourself a valuable resource in a world dictated by a "don't rock the boat" philosophy is a nearly impossible task.

3. *Businesses have become leaner.*

Twenty or twenty-five years ago, it was easy to find organizations with redundant positions. Sometimes this was done deliberately so the business would not suffer if someone

---

[4] Beck, Randall and Harter, Jim, "Why Great Managers Are So Rare," Gallup.com, March 25, 2014, Web, November 15, 2017.

was sick, left, or got promoted. But often this was done in a *de facto* manner. That is, companies hired workers and expected them to stay forever. Likewise, workers found a company and expected to work there forever, take the pension, and live happily ever after. Employees were not simply kicked out the door when their usefulness was questioned.

Unfortunately, due to a multitude of factors, companies now feel the need to run much leaner. Profit margins are thinner and competition is more prevalent. Especially with the advent of online shopping (and price comparison), consumer loyalty is tough to come by. Who wouldn't buy something for 30% less? The old line salespeople have become more accustomed to getting calls from their best, oldest, and most loyal customers that start out something like, "Bill, you know I really like you, but...."

4. *Sometimes the company changes and there isn't much you can do.*

I have observed many companies over the years and one of the interesting things is how companies assume the attitudes of their leadership. I have seen companies go from mission-driven, aggressive organizations to "we've always done it that way" companies fearful to make changes to keep up. And that can happen with just one employee change – the boss.

When a company hires a new employee, especially at higher levels, the new employee knows that he or she is expected to make things better. Status quo is rarely acceptable. The new boss will be on the immediate lookout for underperformers and non-team players (or in reality, what he or she perceives to be an underperformer or non-team player) to make some changes. Right or wrong, that might just be you in his or her eyes.

Something that is often not considered when a new company leader is brought in is this: typically that person was a superstar at another company. That's why he or she was selected to lead your department, division, or organization. But he or she didn't do it alone. Over time a team was built that supported that person and made them successful. And, in the back of your new boss' mind is the idea that if he or she just had a team like they had at the other place, things would be great.

That's another way of saying, new bosses like to bring in their own teams rather than spend the time and effort on developing the talent that is there already.

The bottom line is, in the past, when someone got let go from his or her job, there was a good reason behind it. Maybe they embezzled or lied or cheated somehow. But there was almost always a reason. There was also a stigma. If you lost your job, YOU did something wrong. In the end, it was YOUR fault.

Today, that stigma still persists, but often it is in the mind of the job seeker much more than of his friends and family. As we will learn later, many people go through this trial in their career, some multiple times, through no fault of their own. And even though it is hard to admit it has happened to you, many others see no negative aura around you because you lost a job. Indeed, as you will also see in this book, there are many, many people willing to help you!

All that information may make you feel a little better, and I hope it does. But don't just take my word for it. Let's look to medicine for advice.

Many people go through this trial in their career, some multiple times, through no fault of their own. And even though it is hard to admit it has happened to you, many others see no negative aura around you because you lost a job. Indeed, as you will also see in this book, there are many, many people willing to help you!

In 1969, a Swiss psychiatrist published a book entitled *On Death and Dying.*[5] The book was inspired by the doctor's work over the

[5] Kubler-Ross, Elisabeth, On Death and Dying, New York, The McMillan Company, 1969, Print.

years with terminally ill patients. Since then, Elisabeth Kubler-Ross' model outlining the five stages of grief has become a model for developing coping skills. Interestingly, over time, practitioners and lay people alike have discovered that virtually any major loss in a person's life will result in a progression through Kubler-Ross' five stages model.

The loss of a job is certainly a major life blow and, as such, is no exception!

The Kubler-Ross Five Stages of Grief

1. *Denial*

   Kubler-Ross defined the first stage, denial, as the stage in which the individual affected believes there has been a mistake. They cling to a false reality, or a sense that this error will be corrected somehow.

   Denial is a very common reaction among those who lose jobs. The United States is somewhat unique in the importance and self-value we associate with our jobs. Often the first question asked of a new acquaintance is, "What do you do?" In other countries, that question is virtually never asked and may even be considered rude. Yet we use that inquiry to learn the initial facts about a person we meet.

   After an unexpected job loss, it is not uncommon for a person to continue to say they are working at their previous employer, at least for awhile. This can avoid the awkward situation when someone asks what we do for a living. I have even worked with job search candidates who refused to tell their spouse and family about the situation, packing up the car and leaving each morning as if nothing had changed, only to go to the library or coffee shop to make phone calls and peruse job boards.

   As you think back on the accomplishments in your previous job, which you will do in building your resume, etc., you may well convince yourself that your company will see the error of its ways and come crawling back. I've actually seen that happen, but not very often. Chances are they won't. And, chances are very good that you will end up better off if they don't.

2. *Anger*

The stage of anger involves quite a bit of internal questioning. "How can this happen to me? I'm a good person!" "Who can I blame for this? This can't be my fault!" "How can they get rid of me when the company is full of worthless people who don't earn their keep?"

These are all good questions. And after years of working with job seekers who ask these very questions, the only answer I can provide is, "I don't know." You may never know either. And that's ok.

The anger stage actually serves a very valuable purpose in the process of getting over a job loss. While early on you will likely feel as if it has all been a big mistake and they will come crawling back to you, by going through the process of anger, you will soon realize that you don't want them to come looking for you. Groucho Marx was famous for saying that he had no interest in belonging to a club that would have him as a member. That same logic prevails here. You will find that you don't want to work there anymore!

It's time to move on.

3. *Bargaining*

The bargaining stage for those who have lost jobs often includes some self-blame, rightly or wrongly. Even though you don't know of anything you did wrong, you want to identify the cause and, once identified, change that behavior.

For example, maybe your last performance appraisal had a comment about your missing a few meetings. This may have nothing to do with the real reason you were let go (remember, often it wasn't really anything you did), but since that's the only concrete behavior you can identify, you key in on that and promise yourself that, in your next job, you will be the most punctual, diligent meeting attender ever. By cleaning up your act (you believe), you will be the perfect employee that no other organization could pass up!

It's normal to want to attach causes to explain effects. We all do it. In the perfect world, if we do good things, good things happen. Unfortunately, this world is far from perfect.

As you work your way through the bargaining stage, you will come to realize, you are pretty good just the way you are.

4. *Depression*

Depression (the feeling of despair, hopelessness, and the lack of enjoyment of typically enjoyable activities) is often expected among those who lose jobs. A 2014 Gallup Poll of over 18,000 unemployed adults concluded that unemployed Americans are more than twice as likely to report that they have or are currently being treated for depression.[6] Surprisingly, depression may hit younger workers too, and even harder. In fact, the Centers for Disease Control in 2010 released a study showing that exact correlation. The report showed that the odds of depression were about three times higher for unemployed than employed adults. That report focused on "emerging adults" defined as between ages eighteen and twenty-five.[7]

---

[6] Crabtree, Steve, "In US, Depression Rates Higher for Long-Term Unemployed," Gallup.com, June 9, 2014, Web, November 15, 2017.
[7] "BRFSS 2010 Survey Data and Documentation." CDC.gov/brjss/annual_data/annual_2010.htm, June 23, 2014, Web, November 15, 2017.

5. *Acceptance*

Thankfully, at one pace or another, we eventually reach a stage of acceptance. This stage involves the embrace of the inevitable ("I'm going to have to find another job."). The acceptance stage is accompanied by a feeling of calm, an ability to examine the past more objectively, and a stability of emotions.

For job seekers, this stage is where the work really begins!

Elisabeth Kubler-Ross became well-known for her theory of the five stages outlined here. However, later in her life she made a very important discovery that is often overlooked. She actually claimed that she regretted publishing them in such a concrete order. She noted that, while most people go through all five stages in the event of a major life issue, people do not always go through them in a linear fashion. One may start with depression, then move to denial. Another may begin with bargaining, then anger. Further, the stages are rarely of a predictable length and may be revisited. A long-term job seeker may experience depressive episodes multiple times, for example.

You will undoubtedly experience many or all of the five stages of grief. That's okay. It is not only understandable, it is expected and will actually help you get through the emotional aspects of what is happening. There is nothing wrong with feeling the way you feel. You are fine just the way you are!

Staying Motivated

One of the obstacles you will face in your job search is staying motivated. You will receive rejections, including ones that you never saw coming, and a few of those will have you throwing your hands up in disgust and asking, "What's the use?" The lure of the uncut yard or the couch with the television remote on it will begin to look more and more attractive.

The problem is that a job is not going to come to you. Your new job is a function of your activity and good activity means you must be motivated!

In the coming chapters, I will be helping you develop a plan. That plan will be your roadmap to your next job. While working on your roadmap you will frequently feel as though you have made no progress, but you have. Much of the job search process involves sowing seeds and taking steps that are difficult to see. I will help you develop a team of people who will work on your behalf so that your job search is continuing even when you aren't necessarily working on it.

Everything you do in your job search is taking you closer to that next position, whether you believe it or not.

In my work, I have identified three keys that you can use to help keep yourself motivated in your job search. They may not seem likely to work as you read them, but, believe me, they will be an invaluable way for you to keep going.

The Three Keys to Motivation

1. *Working Your Plan.*

   Once we have developed your plan and you are comfortable with how it works and how to work it, you will find that, during times when you are lost, discouraged, and unmotivated, simply completing a step or two of your plan will lift your spirits. Sending an email, making a call, or scheduling a meeting can all make you feel much better about your chances. I have seen dozens of people go from virtually no prospects to a great new job in a couple of DAYS just because they made another contact, applied for one more job, or updated their LinkedIn profile.

2. *Informational Meetings*

There was a time, believe it or not, when you anxiously awaited the Sunday newspaper because that was when the best job opportunities were published in the classified section. There were pages and pages of potential jobs listed each week. Typically in alphabetical order, they were there for you to circle the best ones for you, followed up by letters, phone calls, or whatever method was recommended for expressing interest.

Those days are gone.

Now, posted jobs are listed electronically on job boards like Indeed, Monster, Ladders, Career Builder, and company-specific websites. And since it is so easy for anyone with a computer and internet connection to find them, the best jobs are inundated with applicants. You will learn later, while people do get jobs by applying through job boards, that is not the most efficient way to do so. In fact, the online site Glassdoor reports that the average corporate job opening now attracts 250 resumes.[8] How can you make yourself stand out?

The answer is the informational meeting.

And the good news is that I will teach you how to obtain, conduct, and leverage those informational meetings in this book. It is a fact that holding an informational meeting will bolster your job search confidence!

3. *Trust the Process*

The process I am going to teach you will work. While others may promise you a job in two weeks or two months, I can't do that. The fact is that it takes longer for some people to find a job than others. But following the process will result in a job.

---

[8] "Top HR Statistics," Glassdoor.com/employers/popular-topics/hr-stats.htm, publication date unknown, Web, November 15, 2017.

Dealing with Rejection

One of the most important facts you must face early on is that you will receive rejections. You will get rejected when all you have done is apply for a job; you will get rejected after one, two, or four interviews; you may get rejected for the job you convinced yourself was yours.

Let's take some time even before we get rolling on the job search to look at how and why those rejections come, what they mean, and what to learn from them, if anything.

First of all, when you apply for jobs online, the typical response you will get is not a rejection. It is silence! Sometimes you may receive an email saying they received your application and they will determine if you are a good fit and contact you if you are. But, if that earlier statistic from Glassdoor is true, and a company interviews the top four candidates, your chances of hearing something positive (or anything at all) from that application is 1.6%. Do not be surprised when you hear nothing.

Later on, we'll talk about something called an applicant tracking system that almost all companies use now, and why you don't hear back will make much more sense.

> *One of the most important facts you must face early on is that you will receive rejections. You will get rejected when all you have done is apply for a job, you will get rejected after one, two, or four interviews. You may get rejected for the job you convinced yourself was yours.*

If you do hear back, since only one person will ultimately get the job, the chance that you are getting the offer is now one in 250, or 0.4%.

Those odds are pretty depressing, admittedly. But remember, online job seeking is one of the least efficient ways to get a job. We will be concentrating on methods that are much more efficient in the coming pages. So don't despair!

The truth is, just as there are reasons you lost your job that aren't your fault, there are plenty of reasons you are receiving a rejection that are not your fault as well. Here are some thoughts on rejections that may help you keep them in perspective.

The Job Was Never Really Available

In larger companies especially, all jobs are posted internally and externally. You, as a job seeker, have no way to tell if the position is already promised to someone internally, or, as often happens, if someone has already been tentatively offered the job. Larger companies must prove that they are complying with certain non-discrimination guidelines and they often post all jobs to show that they are not discriminating. So you have no chance from the start!

Unfortunately, without an inside source feeding you information (which I will help you develop later), there is no way for you to know whether or not a job posting is real.

There Isn't a Good Reason

Managers are people too. They make decisions on instinct sometimes, and the results may not make any sense to anyone else. The hiring manager may simply feel that another candidate is a better "cultural" fit for the organization. Another employee may have recommended a friend and given a glowing review that swayed the decision.

They Are Hiding Behind the Law

All companies in the U.S. are subject to equal employment opportunity laws, the largest of which is called Title VII of the Civil Rights Act of 1964. This law provides protection from discrimination in hiring (and employment practices) for a wide range of "classes," including sex, race, national origin, religion, and others. There are similar laws aimed at protecting against age discrimination for those over forty and workers with disabilities.

These laws form the basis for many lawsuits annually against companies. These suits claim a variety of allegations of discrimination in the hiring process, the promotion process, terminations, and everything else under the sun. Defending these cases – even if unproven and undeserved – is very costly for companies. Indeed, many are settled rather than tried simply because it is the cheaper option.

Consequently, companies are very hesitant to give any information to the non-selected candidates about the decision. Most commonly, a seemingly cold-hearted email is sent simply saying that the company is pursuing other candidates with no further reasoning given or offered.

You may have been a great candidate. You may have been the runner up. It may have, literally, come down to a coin toss. But you will never know. And your mind will likely begin telling you all the things that were wrong with you. In reality, you might have almost gotten the job, beating out hundreds of others! You just don't know.

The true fact is there are many reasons you might not get a job, no matter how perfect you felt you were for it, that have literally nothing to do with you or your qualifications. Among those are:

1. An internal candidate was targeted all along and the posting of the job was only done to satisfy some compliance requirement. The company might not even have looked at outside resumes - including yours.
2. The job description was written by someone in HR that is unfamiliar with the job. So the description that sounded so perfect for you wasn't a true reflection of what the hiring manager really wanted.
3. You are so well-qualified for the position that the hiring manager felt threatened.
4. Your wealth of relevant experience was interpreted that you would want too much money.
5. You are qualified for the job opening that was published, but the hiring manager changed the spec dramatically.

Perhaps she decided she wanted someone with a professional designation or more years of experience.

6. You are qualified, but the keyword searching algorithm the company uses (in the applicant tracking system) is not set to select qualified candidates correctly.

7. You are highly qualified, but you are missing one small item that some company bureaucrat decided was a "must-have" for the job, even though it really wasn't.

8. The HR staffer or hiring manager has an "ideal" candidate in mind in terms of age, gender, experience, etc., and you are not what they envisioned. (Yes, discrimination is illegal, but it does happen, consciously and unconsciously.)

9. The screener cannot make the connection between your relevant experience in another industry and the industry in which they are hiring.

10. The HR screener or hiring manager may simply have a bias against people who are out of work.

11. You are qualified, but the hiring manager went with an old friend. Or, perhaps, someone higher in the organization referred someone and the hiring manager felt obligated to go with that person to keep on good terms with the boss.

12. You are qualified, but the hiring manager is trying to find a bargain, i.e., someone who will do the job well below market value.

The common characteristic in all ten examples: you are qualified, and you could have done the job!

A rejection of your application is not a rejection of you, your abilities, your honor, or your integrity. It is just someone's opinion and nothing more. It's extremely hard, but do not take rejections personally.

Exercise: Developing Your Personal Plan to Handle Rejection

Remember, a job search is a process and chances are you won't land a job in your preferred timing. And rejection is, unfortunately, just part of the process and likely is no reflection on you and your abilities.

To better handle the inevitable rejections, develop your own personal plan by completing the following:

1. Read and reread the list of twelve reasons qualified applicants don't get the job in this chapter. When you receive a rejection, review the list and identify all of the potential reasons you were rejected.

2. Acknowledge the feelings you have when you receive a rejection but tell yourself that each rejection brings you closer to that offer. Accept it as part of the process.

3. Do something good for yourself when you receive a rejection. Exercise is an excellent, proven remedy to depression and despair. Plus, it's a good way to take out your disappoint!

4. In this book you will be encouraged to set goals for networking and applications among other things. When a rejection comes, go back to your goals and start working on them again. It will make you quickly forget the hurt of a rejection.

5. Engage a support group to help each other through rejections. You will be learning about the Team Networking Group program. Involvement in a group with other job seekers allows you to meet others who can help "talk you off the ledge" when needed.

Jeff Echols Story – Conclusion

Upon losing his job, Jeff's first thought, understandably, was, "How do I get another one?" He had no resume and no current job seeking experience or expertise.

Almost immediately, Jeff had an idea. He was going to begin aggressively networking. He was going to meet a new person every day for coffee. In fact, he was going to document each one of the coffee meetings and post information about the person he met and what the person does on social media. Soon, Jeff's new initiative had a name: coffee a day. It also quickly had a website: www.coffeeaday.net.

To date, Jeff has held over 250 coffee a day meetings and is now developing a podcast to go with the website.

On the job front, Jeff immediately reached out to an architect friend who told him to send a resume. The only thing Jeff had resembling a resume was a list of his projects. He submitted, in effect, a twenty-page resume!

The annual AIA national convention was also just around the corner. Jeff was a regular attendee but, of course, that was easy when his firm was paying the registration fee and hotel bills. He discussed with his wife whether he should spend the money to go. She answered his question by asking, "Can you afford not to?" Jeff contacted the AIA and found that he could offset his fees by volunteering. He signed up for anything and everything, eventually getting his entire fee waived. He found a roommate to share a hotel with to cut the cost and drove the six hours to Atlanta to save on airfare.

While there, Jeff was introduced to someone who was starting a new venture that offered various business services to architecture firms nationally. Soon, Jeff was employee #1, although just part-time.

His twenty-page resume also paid off, as he was eventually hired as the director of membership development for the Indiana AIA – again, part-time.

Today, Jeff spends about 25% of his time at the business he connected with in Atlanta, about 50% of his time with the AIA, and the remainder as a sought-after consultant to architecture firms on marketing. This year, things have come full circle as he was asked to be a keynote speaker at the AIA national convention – all expenses paid plus a handsome speaking fee!

CHAPTER FIVE

Taking Stock

After a long career, Tim found himself on the outside looking in. Tim had been with a large pharmaceutical company for his entire career, over twenty-five years. And when the company decided to trim its workforce and Tim was let go, he was in his fifties and not at all ready to retire.

Tim was certain that his future would be in a similar company, perhaps with a competitor or a supplier to his old employer, somewhere he could put his quarter century of industry knowledge to work.

He applied for a few jobs with those companies but also applied to one that was way outside his target industries. Amazingly, he got that job and is now the president of the Better Business Bureau in a large Midwestern city.

How did Tim the pharma guy land a plum job with an organization that is miles away from his past? The answer is simple: transferable skills.

Tim had held several positions during his time at his previous company, and his last role involved frequent contact with politicians and office holders at the county, city, state, and even federal levels. Not-for-profit organizations like the BBB must maintain excellent relationships with governmental and other officials, as lobbying and fundraising are two key components of the organization's success.

Tim already knew the power players in those positions, and the board of directors for the BBB jumped on him for their newest leader.

Many job seekers get tunnel vision when it comes to looking for the next position. They assume that the next one will be very similar to the last one. More precisely, most job seekers pigeonhole themselves in their own minds, telling themselves (and prospective employers) that they are what they were. If you were a banker, you are likely to tell prospective employers and network contacts that you are still a banker. If you were a teacher in a high school, you will call yourself a high school teacher.

You may not be connected to government officials like Tim, but you certainly have skills that you have developed to a very high level in your previous position that other employers will find valuable.

Banking involves many different facets such as financial and budget controls, high-level compliance, auditing, mortgage lending, financing. The list goes on. Believe me, there are companies out there (other than banks) that want and need people with that type of experience. Teaching isn't just about standing in front of a bunch of teenagers and talking for six or seven hours a day. You have amazing experience in organizational development (creating training plans), training and development, and, most important, you are an expert at explaining things to others in an understandable and applicable way. Financial companies, marketing firms, and training consultants all need someone like you!

> *The ability to identify your transferable skills and to broaden your target positions, both in terms of the position itself and the type of company, can significantly reduce your job search duration.*

So, then, the question becomes, what transferable skills do you have? First, allow yourself to recognize that you do have valuable transferable skills. As a new job seeker, you may have difficulty remembering anything that you really did during those last ten years. You may also fall into the common trap of thinking that if you can do it, anyone can. That's just not true. You have a unique combination of education and experience paired with particular skills that you mastered and demonstrated. The trick is to first give yourself enough freedom to recognize them and second, to methodically identify them.

Three Steps to Discovering Your Transferable Skills

1. *What do you love to do?*

Have you ever heard the old saying that if you do what you love you will never work a day in your life? That may be trite but it rings true. If you are an avid golfer, you probably jump out of bed on Saturday and Sunday, maybe even earlier than you did during the week for work. There is no hitting the snooze button and you are never, ever late to meet the rest of your foursome at the course. Wouldn't it be great if you found a job that brought out that type of passion in you?

Foremost, despite the rampant cries of TGIF workers at week's end and the typical stereotype of people being completely miserable at their job, there are people out there who love what they do. They are the lucky ones. But nothing says that you can't join that club with your next position.

But not everyone can be a professional golfer playing day after day after day, right? Right. But there is a lot more to the game of golf than being a professional player. Country clubs employ everyone from instructors to facilities and fleet managers, from club managers to event coordinators and planners.

The key to going from that job you tolerated in corporate America to working in the golf industry you are passionate about? Transferable skills!

In the coming paragraphs, I am going to encourage you to make lists of things you enjoy, are good at, are known for. But this isn't an exercise you should plan to complete in the next ten minutes. I understand you are anxious to get going and find your next job, but contemplation about your answers is crucial. So be patient and take this very seriously. Start by thinking of the things that you love to do. Don't limit it to what you liked at your last job. Similarly, don't limit it to what you like to do outside of work. Everything is in bounds for these exercises. Broaden your thinking!

Bruce Flanagan, a Career Coach and staff member of an excellent organization called Passport to Employment, a ministry of an Indianapolis-area church devoted to helping job seekers, presents it this way: "What was the last thing you were doing when you lost track of time? What were you working on when you realized you forgot to stop for lunch or looked up and realized it was dark outside?" Most likely, you were doing something you love to do.

Chances are you will have no problem identifying something you love to do very quickly. Maybe it's a sport like tennis. Perhaps you are quilter or you just can't volunteer enough at your church. It could be that you feel most at home when volunteering at the adult day care center helping the elderly.

In reality, we all have more than one thing that we love to do. One of my passions is the prison ministry with which I am involved. I am always thinking of ways I can better help the offenders and ex-offenders lead better lives. My wife and I also enjoy traveling, mostly to warm climates, a couple times a year. Along with my life's calling of helping job seekers, those are two examples of things I love doing.

Begin your list of your favorite activities and pay special attention over the next few days and weeks for things that get your heart racing!

2. *What are you good at?*

Sometimes people are lucky enough to find that the skills they are best at are also the ones they love the most. That makes sense, since we tend to like things that we are really good at. But that correlation isn't always the case. With some introspection, you may find that clues have been all around you of things that you are really good at but just never picked up on them.

Did your former boss often tap you to make presentations? If so, there is a reason. You are probably an excellent presenter. Transferable skill! Were you asked to facilitate the discussions at staff meetings? Transferable skill! Have people told you that you are very easy to talk to? Transferable skill! Did that new accounts payable system seem to make sense to you before anyone else last year? Transferable skill!

All through your life people have told you that you are good at different things. You may not have really heard them or perhaps you just didn't believe them, but they were pointing out your transferable skills, skills that you should be playing up when you are applying for jobs, especially jobs in other industries.

Different things come more easily to different people. Whatever it is that comes easy to you is probably a valuable, transferable skill. One of my TNG members is a master at taking tests. In his industry, he earned a dozen professional designations and licenses, most of which were not required for his position. Where's the transferable skill? He is now an instructor, teaching others to take professional tests more successfully. What comes easy to you? Transferable skill!

3. *What personal qualities do you have?*

Luckily, in this world, we are all unique. We may look similar and even sound the same, but no two of us is exactly alike. Each of us has certain qualities that make us who we are. And in those differences lies the potential to find more transferable skills.

Research indicates that about half of the people in the world are introverts (we are all a combination of both introversion and extroversion, so it's really hard to say for sure). Introverts get their strength from solitude and need time to think. Even though an introvert may be a fixture at all the best parties and functions, they need time to recover afterwards. This also means that half the people in the world are not naturally comfortable with networking. Extroverts get their energy from being around others. They want to meet and engage. They can't stand to be alone for long. If your personality type is more extroverted, this desire (need!) to engage others can be a very powerful transferable skill.

Psychologists tend to identify five basic personality traits and categorize them with the acronym OCEAN.[9] Some maintain that there are actually hundreds of personality traits, but, in reality, they all likely fall under the big five. O stands for "open to new experiences." If you have this personality trait, it means you enjoy new things. You have a vivid imagination, tend to enjoy and engage in art and artistic pursuits, experience intense emotions, need variety to thrive, and like complex issues rather than simple, straightforward ones. I bet you can think of many types of companies and roles that would be perfect for an outgoing, artistic person who likes variety and complexity.

C is for conscientiousness. Conscientious people are highly organized and methodical, and they tend to work until the to-do list is finished. Individuals with high conscientiousness complete tasks and do them successfully, appreciate order and systems, follow the rules, and work hard. They are self-disciplined and have little need for micro-managing. They are their own harshest critic. They also tend to be careful and avoid mistakes. Again, how many organizations would not be thrilled to get a hard worker who doesn't need supervision and rarely makes errors?

E stands for extroversion. Although we touched on this earlier, in more scientific terms, extroverts are generally warm people who make friends easily and love parties – the bigger the better! Extroverts are known to take charge, stay busy, and love exciting, fast-paced environments. They also exude positive emotions and are generally optimistic. Many of the factors of an extrovert are what companies often say they are looking for in leaders!

A indicates agreeableness. These people are about trust, honesty, and tolerance. They get along with others extremely well. Building

[9] Berman, Robby, "The Big Five Personality Traits and What They Mean to Psychologists," http://bigthink.com/robby-berman/the-5-personality-types-and-why-you-care, April 27, 2017, Web, November 15, 2017.

relationships is most important to these people. In more particular terms, agreeable people trust others, value compliance (they don't cheat or take shortcuts), work hard to make others feel welcome, and are easy to satisfy. They are much more comfortable letting the light shine on others and remaining in the background. And they sympathize with others. Doesn't that sound like someone who would make a great HR professional? Or a top-notch executive assistant?

The final letter in the acronym is N for Neuroticism. Before you panic and get defensive claiming you are not neurotic, when psychiatrists and psychologists use the term, it is not necessarily indicating anything negative. It is simply a characteristic that makes you, you. Neurotics are worriers and more pessimistic. They may get frustrated and angry more easily and could overreact to situations. Sounds like the perfect quality manager or auditor to me!

Transferable skills are everywhere! But you have to be in the right mindset to look for and identify them. Just about any trait you have, just about any activity you love and/or are good at, can be a skill that might help you get your next job.

Transferable skills are everywhere!

Personality Assessments

There is another approach to identifying some of your transferable skills that is much more methodical and some of you (especially you conscientious ones!) may find easier and quite valuable. Over the past few years, several scientifically-based assessments have been developed that have shown to be statistically valid in helping you learn more about yourself and your traits.

One of the most popular tools on the market today is called Strengthsfinder. It is owned by the Gallup company, famous for surveys. You can access the Strengthsfinder exam online for $19.99 or, as most people prefer, you can purchase the book by the same name, which will include a one-time use code for you to take the online exam. The cost of the exam is included in the price of the book.

By purchasing the book, you get not only the exam but also lots of information about the interpretation of the exam. I recommend the book. However, don't make the mistake of getting it at the library or buying it used. Someone else will have used the code and it won't work twice.

Strengthsfinder identifies thirty-four different areas of aptitude through a series of seemingly unrelated questions. You will have to choose between statements such as "I love to study" and "I live to go out." Or "I am a very private person" versus "My life is an open book." Once the test is completed, you will receive a list of your top five areas of strength along with strategies that you can use to capitalize on those strengths.

Strengthsfinder is well known in the business world and most likely will carry some weight in an interview if you were to bring it up and discuss your top skills with a prospective employer.

While Strengthsfinder is an excellent resource to help you identify those transferable skills, it is definitely not the only option. There are several other, less well-known exams that you can take for free. I've listed several in the following pages.

Myers-Briggs Type Indicators (MBTI®) (myersbriggs.org)

The *Myers-Briggs Type Indicator (MBTI®)* assessment is one of the world's most popular personality tools, used widely in business and people development globally. With more than 70 years of science-based, research-based insight, the MBTI assessment is a robust tool for self-awareness and improvement. It can provide perspective on your personality type, how you're "wired", and positive language for understanding individual characteristics and strengths drawn from your personality type. The reports help you identify areas of strength, potential challenges and strategies, and over 20 job families/career options ranked by how they are particularly suited to your personality. It's often used in personal development, leadership training, career change, and transitions.

The Myers-Briggs assessment is available from certified

practitioners, who have a background or training in psychology, and/or have passed the publisher's qualifications. It begins with an extensive questionnaire to investigate your preferences across a wide range of behavior and situations. Then, the practitioner reviews the report with you for insights and strategies.

You'll notice some of the other assessment tools mentioned, use the Myers-Briggs model and terminology as a baseline. So there is value in using the original instrument itself. Career coaches and career counselors are often certified in the Myers-Briggs instrument.

Strong Interest Inventory (careerassessmentsite.com/tests/strong-tests)

The *Strong Interest Inventory* assessment helps individuals identify their work personality by exploring their interests in six broad areas or Themes, and draws out areas of interest, preferred work activities, characteristics, areas of skill, work style, and values. These are then mapped to 130 occupations (jobs) and ranked by degree of potential "fit". The *Strong* assessment heightens people's self-awareness and provides deeper understanding of individual strengths and blind spots, including work style and orientation to risk taking, backed by more than 80 years of research into how people of similar interests are employed, and what motivates individuals in the workplace.

The *Strong* helps you align your interests with areas of responsibility and where those interests can be applied. It offers insights into career exploration, career development, and career transition. It's provided by the same publisher as the Myers-Briggs assessment, and is also available from certified practitioners, and begins with a questionnaire. The practitioner reviews the report with you for insights and strategies.

Career coaches and career counselors are often certified in both the Myers-Briggs and *Strong* instruments – some use one or the other based on the client's level of career experience, others prefer to use both. They help you with observations and perspectives the tools bring out, that you might pass over on your own.

Discover Your Skills (discoveryourskills.com)

This website was created with the assistance of Mike Rowe, famous for hosting Dirty Jobs on the Discovery Channel. Mike is a passionate champion of helping young people find their ideal careers to be happy and successful in life and this site is designed with that end in mind. The test can be taken by anyone but is geared toward those just starting out or those wanting to make a career/industry change.

Free Aptitude Test (richardstep.com/richardstep-strengths-weaknesses-aptitude-test/)

The Richard Step organization offers a free aptitude test that will take just a few minutes to complete and return your top three strengths as well as your biggest weakness.

41 Questions (41q.com)

41 Questions is based on the Myers-Briggs personality Inventory that has been used in businesses for decades. This site will give you a general description of yourself but will also offer a more complete version for a price.

Human Metrics (humanmetrics.com/cgi-win/jtypes2.asp)

Human Metrics is another site based on the Myers-Briggs inventory. This site will give you a more complete report than 41 Questions and is still free.

Red Bull Wingfinder (wingfinder.com)

The catchphrase for Red Bull's energy drink is it "gives you wings." And they have backed this up by co-developing an online test called Wingfinder. This test was developed and tested by a team of psychology professors from the University of London and Columbia University in New York. According to the site, it "focuses on your strengths, the things that you are naturally inclined to be good at, and gives you the tools and coaching to be even better."

You are so much more than your last job! Finding your transferable skills, your passion, and your innate abilities will allow you to see job opportunities that you never considered before!

Exercise: Identify Your Top Ten Transferable Skills

When I was interviewing candidates for positions during my career, one of my favorite requests was for them to list the top ten skills they could bring to the position. Frankly, that was a tough question for most people as the most common responder could only list two or three at best.

But I also found that this exercise is invaluable for job seekers. First, it prepares them if they may encounter that or a similar question. Second, it forces them to make the effort to identify and analyze their transferable skills. On top of that, it often makes them better candidates because the self-examination necessary to complete the exercise serves to build their confidence.

For this chapter, complete as many of the assessments mentioned above and read the results carefully. Then, using the space below, list your top ten transferable skills and commit them to memory.

My Top Ten Transferable Skills

1.

2.

3.

4.

PART 3

LEARNING THE TOOLS AND TECHNIQUES

TNG Strategy: Providing support to our members
is only helpful when paired with the latest
tools, techniques, and strategies that we
teach to find a job. These methods will result
in a shorter, more productive job search!

CHAPTER SIX
Today's Job Search

Technology was going to make our life easier, remember? According to the Jetsons, we would have robot maids and flying cars by now! Productivity was going to skyrocket, paper was going to be obsolete, and the majority of our time would be spent in leisure.

Of course, none of that has happened, although technology has made our lives different and, in many ways, improved them. Smartphones can be used for everything from ordering a car to learning a new language. Televisions an inch thick bring you hundreds of channels and even allow you to rearrange the offerings to fit your schedule. Our cars are more sophisticated than the Apollo 11 mission to the moon, giving us real time directions, helping us avoid traffic jams, and even parking for us.

Yes, technology has made our lives at least more interesting, if not easier.

But if you are a job seeker, you will likely find that technology has made the entire process both foreign and inefficient. Most of all, you are likely to find it incredibly frustrating!

Nick Corcodilos has been a headhunter in Silicon Valley for almost forty years, so he has seen the system change and change again. Nick hosts an online column entitled "Ask the Headhunter," and in a 2013 issue he argued that HR should actually get out of the hiring business! Those sound like "fightin' words" to most HR professionals. He blames much of the current frustration with the HR function squarely on the HR departments themselves. For example, HR departments rarely respond to job applicants unless they want to schedule an interview – phone or in person. When asked why, most say they don't have time because they are inundated with applicants. When one asks why they are inundated, the answer is that they post jobs on multiple job boards, inviting anyone who can "press an enter key to apply!"[10]

The AARP, American Association of Retirement Persons, expends substantial time and energy to help its members (who can be as young as fifty) find new jobs if they aren't ready to fully retire. In July 2016, AARP published an article online explaining how the job search has changed. The contrast is pretty remarkable. Many of those under thirty or thirty-five will not remember when things were considerably different. But those over forty certainly will.[11]

Then: Newspaper ads were the primary source of job listings. Now: Millions of job postings appear online every day.

As Nick Corcodilos pointed out, electronic job boards like Indeed, Monster, Career Builder, and hundreds of others have made it incredibly easy for a job seeker to find openings. Unfortunately, it has become incredibly easy for everyone else to do the exact same thing, for the same reason. It is even worse because technology has also made it easier to apply once a job is found. In fact, some jobs let people apply simply by sending their LinkedIn profile to the company – with literally one click.[12] Twenty years ago, a job seeker had to invest time in printing a resume, putting it in envelope,

---

[10] www.asktheheadhunter.com
[11] "How Job Hunting Has Changed," https://www.aarp.org/content/dam/ arp/work/ job_hunting/2014-12/How-job-hunting-has-changed-tip-sheet-AARP-PDF.PDF, AARP.org, November, 2014, Web, November 15, 2017.
[12] Corcodilas, Nick, "Why HR Should Get Out Of The Hiring Business," www. asktheheadhunter.com/6249/why-hr-should-get-out-of-the-hiring-business, April 1, 2013, Web, November 15, 2017.

and mailing it. Today I can apply to a hundred jobs in a day with absolutely no cost – or risk – to myself.

Then: Resumes were on paper.
Now: Resumes are electronic.

Paper resumes used to be a sort of art form. Job seekers would try odd-sized paper, colored paper, or anything else they could think of to stand out and grab the attention of the hiring manager. The office supply store even stocked "resume" paper, typically a very thick, high-cotton content paper supposed to show a hiring manager the pride the applicant put into his or her work.

Now, when it comes to resumes, technology is the great equalizer. It doesn't matter what color your resume is or the stock of paper you use. Your resume will be scanned by a computer, reduced to a few fields it deems important, and passed to someone in HR (hopefully) or simply ignored completely (likely). Nothing except the right words and phrases will get you a look.

Then: A real person read your resume.
Now: An applicant tracking system will scan your resume before anyone sees it ... if anyone does see it.

This is the most difficult change for job seekers: the applicant tracking system, or ATS.

Twenty years ago, some of the largest companies were experimenting with ATS technology but today it is accessible and used by virtually every company of any size. Although there are various versions available, they all function similarly. ATS systems compare your application (usually with information culled (or parsed, in ATS vernacular) from your resume) to a secret list of key words and phrases input by the HR/administrator. The ATS is given certain instructions ahead of time regarding the degree of "match" it finds in any given application. For example, if the instructions are for 80%, only those applications containing the words and phrases that match at least 80% of the secret key words and phrases are then passed on to a real person for review. And that doesn't guarantee an interview or further consideration. It simply means you passed the ATS "test."

Unfortunately, most applications seem to fall into the other option. If, in our example, an applicant only matches 78% of the key words and phrases, the computer discards the application, and no one ever sees that the applicant applied. This process is often called the "black hole" by job seekers. If you apply for a job and never hear anything, it is highly likely that the ATS never passed your application on for consideration. Thus, you were sent into the black hole!

Later in the book we'll talk a bit about some strategies for dealing with ATS systems.

Then: If you applied, you got some response, positive or negative.

Now: Many employers will not even acknowledge your application or do so only with a "stock" email stating that your application was received and they will contact you if they are interested.

There are two forces at work here. First, just as Nick Corcodilos pointed out, HR departments are slammed by the number of resumes they receive for each opening they post. With companies running leaner and leaner, there is simply no way someone can respond to every applicant. Also, companies are increasingly scared of liability claims from job seekers claiming discrimination. To win a discrimination claim, a job seeker must have some information showing that the decision was indeed based on that particular quality of the individual. In other words, if the discrimination claim filed asserts that the company discriminated against the job seeker based on his or her age, then the applicant must have information from the company proving that the decision was truly based on that specific characteristic. If the company provides no information at all, not even a "thanks for applying" response, it is harder for an applicant to claim any nefarious decision making.

Then: You prepared a resume, putting your heart and soul into it, and used it repeatedly.

Now: You customize your resume for the position you are interested in and only list relevant activities and only those from the last ten or fifteen years.

A long resume used to be a badge of honor. If you had enough to fill two pages, or, for the top-level people, even three, you were a force to be reckoned with. In a phrase, experience counted.

Today, companies want to see that you match what they are looking for. No one cares about the job you had ten years ago unless it is relevant to the job open now. In fact, a lengthy job history on a resume was once viewed as a sign of wisdom, and experience was a valuable commodity. Today, however, a lengthy job history is a signal to a recruiter that the person is likely out of touch technologically, unwilling to compromise, and probably expects a great deal in compensation.

Then: You shared lots of personal information on your resume. Now: Minimal personal information should be shared.

There was a time, believe it or not, when putting a picture on a resume was considered a good idea. Full addresses, phone numbers, and all kinds of other identification info was expected. Of course, back then, companies often sent rejection letters, so knowing where to send them was important.

Today, there are three basic reasons not to share much personal information on a resume and/or application. First, as an applicant, you do not want to give the company any reason to discriminate against you. Your picture may reveal your race and gender. Likewise, including the year you graduated high school makes it easy for someone to calculate your age. Both of these pieces of information can be used to discriminate against you in the hiring process.

Second, identity theft is one of the fastest growing crimes. The Federal Trade Commission reports that over seventeen million people in the United States were victims of identity theft in 2014 alone.[13] Consider the information you are asked for when you register for a website. Think of the security questions, like the name of your high school, for example. Those are often on a person's resume and almost always on the application. This makes it even easier for someone to steal your identity.

Even sharing your street address today is often discouraged, although not necessarily for privacy reasons. Some companies have a bias toward local candidates. Seeing that you live an hour or more away, even though you are willing to commute, may get you tossed out before you even have a chance. Let them discover your location after they decide you are the one they want!

Then: The hiring manager was probably older and had been with the company a long time.

Now: You have to go through someone in HR who is probably in his first job out of school and in his early twenties.

Thirty years ago, back when the HR department was still called "personnel," the area mainly facilitated the hiring process. They didn't necessarily get involved in finding and vetting the applicants. Today, that is one of HR's primary functions. Consequently, the HR department is the first line of defense that you must overcome before a hiring manager even sees your application. And that worker in HR, depending on your age of course, may be the age of your children. To them, you may look ancient!

People often gravitate to people most like them. After all, most people think they are really good so finding someone similar to themselves is a good thing, right?

---

[13] "17.6 Million U.S. Residents Experienced Identity Theft in 2014," www.bjs.gov/content/pub/press/vit14pr.cfm, Bureau of Justice Statistics, September 27, 2015, Web, November 15, 2017.

Then: Technology didn't matter much; knowing how to type wasn't even required, unless you were looking for a secretarial position.

Now: If you haven't kept up with technology, you probably won't get through the initial screening.

It is rare today that a job posting doesn't include a requirement that applicants be savvy with Microsoft Office or some of its components, like Word and Excel. Indeed, more and more communication within organizations is done through social media and smartphones. If you don't know how to type, well, you are in trouble in today's tech-heavy world!

The good news is that there are a multitude of options to learn the technology that you haven't kept up with. Unemployment offices routinely offer free classes on Word, Excel, and PowerPoint. There are thousands of organizations offering hands-on classes, for a fee of course. But there are also hundreds of free tutorials available online through YouTube and the software manufacturers websites. The public library will also have some helpful resources.

One sure giveaway that you are not tech-savvy and probably an older job seeker is not to have a LinkedIn account. And that account should be complete with your picture and history on it, with the "URL" or address for your LinkedIn page included on your resume.

Another thing to watch for is your email address. Don't use an inappropriate email address for your job search (hotmama4433@ gmail.com), and also watch what email service you use. Believe it or not, your choice of email provider can date you to a young HR screener. AOL is considered what their grandparents used. Stick to safe ones like Gmail.

Finally, even if you don't plan on using Twitter, set up a Twitter account and put your Twitter name (called your "handle") on your resume. It shows a recruiter you are up to date on technology.

Then: Job interviews were about you and discovering if you were someone who could do the job.

Now: Job interviews are much more complex, involve a much lengthier process, and are all about what you can do, not necessarily what you have done.

It used to be that, when you were called for a job interview, you put on your suit and met for an hour with the hiring manager. The hiring manager tried to see if you had the ability to learn and do a job. That was pretty much it.

Today, expect a minimum of two interviews and sometimes more. I have known job seekers who have endured five or six interviews during the process. And you won't just meet the hiring manager. In fact, the hiring manager might be the second or third person you meet. A phone call ("screen") with HR will usually happen first. This will last fifteen to twenty minutes. During that time, the HR rep will simply be determining if there is anything about you that should immediately disqualify you from the running. Supposing you pass that test, an in-person interview with HR may be next. More people will be deselected at each stage, including this one. Then you might meet with the hiring manager, maybe a meeting with the team you will be working with, and maybe even the hiring manager's boss.

Understandably, a process like this, which requires aligning everyone's schedules, takes a significant amount of time. Not many people get hired quickly anymore. For some, the process can last for months!

Expect a minimum of two interviews and sometimes many more. I have known job seekers who have endured five and six interviews during the process.

Another big difference is the way interviews are conducted. Even though companies often talk about the importance of culture fit for a new hire -- if the new person will get along and agree with the principles of the organization -- interviews are typically all about behavior. Today's interviews are based on a concept called behavioral interviewing.

In behavioral interviewing, the interviewer will ask many questions about how you dealt with situations in your past. A common example is, "Tell me about a time when you disagreed with your boss. What did you do and how did you handle the situation?" The theory behind behavioral interviewing is that the past is a good indicator of your future performance.

To excel in a behavioral interview, there is a process called STAR stories. We'll break those down a little later in the book.

Then: If you wanted to know how to find a job, you asked your parents.

Now: Everyone has opinions on how to find a job. Plus, the internet has thousands of websites and columns dedicated to nothing but job seeking.

I like to say that one of the biggest difficulties in a job search is that you don't know what is going to work for you until it works. Even though applying blindly to jobs posted on job boards is a statistically bad and unproductive strategy, every once in a while, it works. But not for most people. As the saying goes, "Even a blind squirrel finds a nut every once in a while."

> *Everyone you ask to review your resume will tell you to change something, I guarantee it.*

Everyone you ask to review your resume will tell you to change something, I guarantee it. People will tell you to do things differently than you are currently doing virtually every day. I helped a job seeker a few years ago who struggled and struggled with what information he wanted to put on his job search business card. When he finally got it to where he was quite pleased with it, the first person he gave one to responded by telling him that the color he had chosen was all wrong. It wasn't, but it still made the job seeker wonder if he had done something that was going to cost him a job.

Since different strategies and techniques work for different people at different times, no one, including me, can tell you the exact things you should be doing to get your job. But I can tell you that certain things are much more likely to work than others. That's what this book is about! So trust yourself and don't put much stock in what everyone else says.

Then: Finding a job was about your qualifications and your eagerness.

Now: Finding a job is about your skills, your history, and, most importantly, who you know.

You would probably be shocked if I told you that some 85% of jobs are found through networking and not through ads or job boards. But that is true.[14] Implicit in that fact is the requirement that you know people to find the jobs. That's what networking is all about.

Constant and committed networking is most likely the way your next job will come about. It may be because your network alerts you to a position before it is even posted. Or it may be that you hear of a position and you are able to contact someone you know there – someone you met through networking – to get the scoop on the job and, ideally, have that person get your resume to the hiring manager, thereby bypassing the HR gauntlet completely. Or, as happens sometime, a networking meeting may turn into a job interview.

You can never meet too many people in your job search.

Exercise: How Up to Date Is Your Job Search?

You may feel as though the old ways of getting a job worked better and, frankly, you would likely be right. Unfortunately, neither you nor I are in a position to change it. So we have to do our best to be successful working within the current system. In order to enhance your chances of success, use this time to ascertain whether you have

---

[14] Adler, Lou, "New Survey Reveals 85% of All Jobs are Filled Via Networking," www. linkedin.com/pulse/new-survey-reveals-85-all-jobs-filled-via-networking-lou-adler/, LinkedIn, February 29, 2016, Web, November 15, 2017.

addressed all appearances that may indicate to a target company that you might be "out of date."

1. What is the email address you are using for correspondence regarding your job search? Is it appropriate?

   Yes   No

2. Do you have a LinkedIn account? Have you completed the headline and summary fields? Do you have a picture?

   Yes   No

   (We will work more on your LinkedIn profile later in Chapter 9.)

3. Have you created a Twitter account? Is it on your resume along with any other marketing materials? Yes   No

4. Is your resume ATS-friendly? Have you chosen a standard font (like Times New Roman or Arial) that a computer can easily read? Is the formatting clear with plenty of white space?

   Yes   No

5. Have you removed your picture from your resume? Have you taken off your address and only included your email address and phone number?

   Yes   No

6. Do you have eight to ten STAR stories ready to use in a behavioral interview?

   Yes   No

   (STAR stories are covered in Chapter 15.)

7. Have you identified at least three online job boards to consult regularly?

    Yes   No

    (We will also talk more about job boards later. Although they are usually not the best way to get a job, it does happen and they can also help you identify likely target companies and connections.)

8. Are you comfortable with your resume and other materials? Are you confident enough in them to discount other people's opinions when they tell you to change something?

    Yes   No

    If you circled "No" for any of these eight questions, this is an indication that you should take time to address these issues before launching headlong into your job search.

CHAPTER SEVEN
Networking

A re you one of the millions of people who cringes when you hear the word "networking"? There are certainly plenty of individuals who enjoy meeting new people, making connections, and going to all the various networking events that take place. They actually look forward to small talk, speed networking events (think of speed dating), and collecting business cards. But for every one of those, there are a dozen who dread the very thought of networking.

Therein lies the beauty and attraction of the online job application. You can sit in front of your computer, read hundreds of job postings, and apply without ever having to talk to anyone or ask for help. The biggest problem with this approach?

It doesn't work. At least, it doesn't work for most people.

There are people who get their jobs solely through Indeed, LinkedIn Jobs, Career Builder, or some company website. But statistically, they are the minority.

According to Forbes, 85% of people find their next job from networking.[15] This means that only about one in six people find a job by surfing the Internet.

---

[15] Adler, Lou, "New Survey Reveals 85% of All Jobs are Filled Via Networking," www.linkedin.com/pulse/new-survey-reveals-85-all-jobs-filled-via-networking-lou-adler/, LinkedIn, February 29, 2016, Web, November 15, 2017.

> ### *According to Forbes, 85% of people find their next job from networking.*

This statistic is backed up by an organization called Interview Success Formula, which compiled information from the U.S. Bureau of Labor Statistics, The Wall Street Journal, and CNN, among others. The company's research showed that in 2012, 80% of available jobs were never advertised.[16]

This data begs the question, how does one find jobs that aren't advertised?

I'm sorry to say, you do it through networking!

TNG client Tim learned the power of networking first-hand. Tim had been out of work for twelve months and was quite frustrated. He had been hesitant to fully involve his network in his job search, perhaps fearing that his friends and professional colleagues would think less of him due to his unemployment status. Of course, the longer it went on, the less comfortable he felt contacting them.

Finally, Tim decided to mount a true campaign to contact his network, letting them know what was going on and what he was looking for.

Three weeks later, Tim had been offered, and accepted, a job that exceeded the salary in his previous position.

There are multiple reasons a company would not post a job on the popular job boards before filling it. Here are a few:

It costs money.

Although there are some free job posting sites, most of the

---

[16] Smith, Jacquelyn, "7 Things You Probably Didn't Know About Your Job Search," https://www.forbes.com/sites/jacquelynsmith/2013/04/17/7-things-you-probably-didnt-know-about-your-job-search/#1f4777df3811, Forbes, April 17, 2013, Web, November 17, 2017.

popular ones (the ones that job seekers tend to visit) have some cost associated with them. These can range from a few dollars a month to several hundred or more. While that might not sound like much by itself, consider a company that has ten or twenty openings. Companies can pay thousands of dollars a year to list all of the open jobs.

They are flooded with applicants.

The technology that powers job boards certainly has advantages. For the job seeker, it makes finding and applying more convenient. On the other hand, since it is easier to find and apply, job boards are typically flooded with applications, making the job of identifying promising candidates even harder for employers.

In fact, some states require a job seeker to demonstrate that he or she has applied to a certain number of jobs each week to collect unemployment benefits. There is no requirement that the applicant be qualified for the job, only that he apply. Consequently, applicants often apply for jobs for which they aren't qualified or in which they have no interest. This causes more work for the HR folks seeking the best candidates, and makes it tougher for the qualified applicants to stand out.

The best applicants come from other sources.

Several television shows in recent years have begun with the premise of people who don't know each other pairing up or even getting married. One of the reasons these shows fascinate us is because of the unlikelihood that two people who barely know each other will get along long term. Advertising for job applicants is very similar.

After a computer makes the first cut in the applications for a job, someone in the HR department has to make judgments on all the remaining applicants as to whether the person is a good fit for both the job and the company. They also have to predict whether the person will stay in the position and, perhaps, be a good candidate for future promotions. All these decisions are made based on a couple 8 ½ x 11 inch pieces of paper.

Once a few of the applicants are chosen, interviews are scheduled.

During the interviews, the interviewer is tasked with making a decision on whether this person can do the job, fit in, retain the position, learn enough to be promoted, and generally get along with the manager. Considering that an employee spends more (awake) time each week at work than with their spouse, that's a pretty tall order.

In the end, hiring is a lot like getting married after a first date. You spend an hour with the person on their best behavior then commit to them for the long term!

Of course, if you are a hiring manager, there are better ways to fill a position. One is to hire internal candidates with whom you are already familiar. This lessens the risk of a bad decision due to a lack of information.

Another approach is to get referrals from current employees. While the hiring manager may not know the applicant personally, a referral from a current employee often acts as a "seal of approval." Making a positive referral to a hiring manager, in effect, puts the credibility of the referring employee on the line. It's like having a reference that is known to the hiring manager and internal to the company. Those are excellent assets for a job seeker!

Indeed, many companies offer monetary incentives to employees who refer successful candidates for open positions. Companies know that this is a valuable way to identify and hire good candidates. It also means that employees are often eager to make referrals for you. They might make some money!

A final approach is to hire someone you already know. Most of us have contacts in our industries and could think of at least a few people who would be good fits for a job. The longer we have known the person, the more comfortable we are with the decision. Thinking about the marriage analogy, just as the best way to choose a spouse is to spend time with them, the best employees are often those that the hiring manager has known for a long time, sometimes for years.

Although far from scientific, I can tell you that in my experience, the likelihood of hiring the "right" person solely from a stack of applications is less than 50%. The chances of hiring successfully from an employee referral increases to around 80%. My success rate in hiring people I already knew for a position was virtually 100%.

So, most hiring managers approach hiring in, more or less, that order:

- First, they look for internal candidates.
- Second, they consider their friends and contacts.
- Third, they ask for employee referrals.
- Fourth, they post on the company website.

If all of those approaches fail, they pay to post the position on the online job boards or farm the position out to a recruiter.

One important note: larger companies will often post ALL their jobs, even if they have every intention of filling the position internally or already have a favorite candidate in mind. This is done because posting all positions is evidence of compliance with EEOC (Equal Employment Opportunity Commission) rules and regulations. Unfortunately, there is often no way for you as the applicant to tell if the job is really "open" to every applying candidate. That can be quite frustrating as a job seeker.

Becoming a Networker

Ironically, if you are like most people, you will find that you get quite good at networking over the course of a job search. In fact, most people never stop networking even after finding their next position, as they come to realize the power of a strong network. But that is down the road. Right now, just jumping into the shallow end of the networking pool might seem intimidating.

The best networkers learn quickly that networking is not about calling people and asking them for a job. No one wants to do that, and no one wants to have someone contact them for that either. Instead, your networking efforts should follow these guidelines.

1. *Set a plan and work your plan.*

   A structured approach to networking will be much more productive than a haphazard one. Set a goal for the number of networking meetings and/or events you plan on attending each week, and then work to fill your schedule accordingly.

   The best networkers learn quickly that networking is not about calling people and asking them for a job.

2. *Have an agenda.*

   Just as you should have a goal for networking each week, each of your networking activities should have a goal as well. For example, if the activity involves a networking event where there will be many other people, have the goal of meeting and obtaining the business cards of at least five people. Then be sure to follow up with them after the meeting. If your networking activity is a meeting with one other person, go in with the goal of learning about that person, their company, and how they got the job they have now. Be sure to go to the meeting with the idea of getting the names and contact info of more people to talk to as well. (More on that later).

3. *Remember, networking is a job.*

   As you begin your networking journey, you will likely find that there are many sources for networking meetings in your area. You can easily fill your calendar with networking events each week and feel that you are being productive and meeting your goals. However, attending the same meetings over and over again, likely with the same people attending each week, will produce rapidly diminishing returns.

   That is not to say you shouldn't commit to attending meetings and do so on a regular basis. Just don't join ten networking groups, attend each one every week, and call that a success.

Choose a few groups that interest you. Visit each one a couple times and determine which you feel are most valuable. Then, settle on three with the goal that you attend two each week, rotating the third in as you feel like it. Fill the rest of your calendar with individual networking meetings.

Informational Meetings

The basis of effective networking is not – thankfully – attending networking events where you don't know anyone, asking random strangers to meet with you, or even trolling human resources staffers and recruiters. The most efficient and effective use of your networking time will be in informational meetings.

An informational meeting occurs with someone who may be in a position to help you obtain a job in the future, either directly as the hiring manager, or indirectly introducing you to the decision makers. Informational meetings are face-to-face meetings, often held at coffee shops (sometimes at the person's office), and are times when you both can get to know each other. People are much more likely to help and recommend others if they have made a face-to-face, personal connection with them. You can think of informational meetings as sort of pre-job interviews.

The first step in filling your networking calendar with informational meetings is to determine your targets. The best informational meetings will be with people in your profession (or the profession you are focusing on) and/or work at the companies you are targeting. Once your targets are identified, you can contact those people and ask if they would be willing to spend a few minutes chatting with you about what they do, their company, their experience, and any advice they might have for you. Be clear that you are not asking or applying for a job with the person. You are simply requesting information and help. And talking about themselves and helping others are two things that people are generally very willing to do!

The request for an informational interview can be made by phone, through LinkedIn, or by email. Your request should not be too formal and certainly not too generic. Mention the person by name, pay them a compliment if possible, and ask if they would be willing to help.

For example, if you are interested in an informational interview with someone at a new tech company in town that has been getting a lot of press, you might send an email saying:

"Hello, Byron. Congratulations on the new round of funding at Connstat. It certainly sounds like an exciting time. My name is Suzy Jobseeker and I am looking to position myself for jobs at Connstat in the future. I'm not applying for a job right now, just trying to learn as much as I can so I can be successful when the right opportunity appears. Would you have a few minutes for me to take you to coffee and learn more about what it's like to work at Connstat, how you like it, and pick your brain for any advice you might have? I promise I won't take more than twenty minutes and I'll buy the coffee! Would you have some time next week to get together?"

This message is personal, non-threatening, and simply asks for help. You will find that many, many people will be more than willing to meet, talk, and help where they can.

Before we talk about where to find the people you would like to meet, let me outline what is likely to happen as a result of your informational meeting. They won't all go according to plan, and they won't all feel like successes, so be ready. But in the long run, they will help you land that job!

1. The meeting goes well, you learn about the other person, the company, the positions you are interested in, and the other person even offers to introduce you to two more people with whom you should network. This is an excellent outcome, not least because you now have more people to schedule for networking. If everyone you meet introduces you to two other individuals, filling that calendar becomes very easy, very quickly!

2. The person is helpful, answers your questions, but doesn't offer any further advice, help, or connections. Unfortunately, that will happen. Thank them for their time and ask them to keep their ears and eyes open. You might also ask if you can contact them if you hear of an opportunity in their company in the future. Almost no one will tell you no to your face, although the helpfulness they offer when that time comes may not be too helpful.

   In Steve Dalton's excellent book, *The Two Hour Job Search*, he refers to people who are like this as "Obligates." These people will do the minimum to help you but won't necessarily go out of their way to further your cause.[17] You will run into them.

3. The person may simply turn you down and not want to meet. The worst scenario is when a person agrees to meet then just doesn't show up. They simply didn't have the guts to say no. Although that is somewhat rare, it does happen. There isn't much you can do in these cases beyond contact the person and say something must have happened and ask to reschedule – if you think it is worth it (Steve Dalton calls these people "Curmudgeons!").

4. In the ultimate win, the person you are meeting with will like you, know of a job opportunity, and make an introduction with a recommendation to the hiring manager. I have even seen situations in which the person has a job available and the informational interview turns into a job interview! Frankly, these scenarios happen much more often than you would think. Remember, most jobs are never posted, so just because you don't see one on the company website does not mean there isn't a position available.

---

[17] Dalton, Steve, *The Two Hour Job Search: Using Technology to Get the Right Job Faster*, 2012, California, Ten Speed Press, Print.

Because you never know which way an informational interview will go, you should prepare accordingly. Dress appropriately. For many, this means business casual attire, depending on the type of job you are pursuing. Act professionally and choose meeting places appropriate for the meeting. Coffee shops are usually safe. Offering to meet for a beer or at a Hooters may be fine for some people, but I wouldn't recommend it. Bring a folder or portfolio with you, paper and pen to take notes, and your business card. Don't bring a resume, but instead, bring your marketing profile and offer it to the person early in the meeting (Marketing profiles are explained further in Chapter 8.)

Chances are, the person you are meeting with will ask to see a resume. When that happens, simply offer to send it to them via email. This ensures that they can print as many copies as they want, are able to forward it electronically to others and, best of all, gives you their email address to stay in touch!

All this sounds great, but it doesn't mean much if you don't have people to meet with!

There are various ways to secure informational meetings, some being more productive and successful than others. But the most successful strategy, and the one you should start with, is mining your current contacts.

Hopefully you have quite a few connections on LinkedIn by now. LinkedIn is the best place to start. As you will see in Chapter 9, LinkedIn is simply a giant, searchable database. Once you are certain of your target position and have a few companies that sound like good fits, the search function on LinkedIn becomes your holy grail.

At the top of the LinkedIn homepage is a search box. Near that search box is a link that says "advanced search." By clicking on the advanced search function, you can pick and choose your search criteria. For example, if you are looking for a position as a graphic designer, type that into the job title search box and hit enter. You will immediately be presented with a very lengthy list of people with the title "graphic designer." The beauty of this list is that your first-degree connections – those people you are directly connected to on

LinkedIn and, presumably, already have a relationship with -- will appear at the top. These are your prime candidates to contact for informational interviews!

Think about it. If someone you used to work with or went to school with and with whom you are connected on LinkedIn sent you a message asking to meet for coffee for advice, would you turn them down? Pretty unlikely. This group is the one most likely to become your champions and help you. Start with them!

> **If someone you used to work with or went to school with and with whom you are connected to on LinkedIn sent you a message asking to meet for coffee for advice, would you turn them down? Pretty unlikely.**

You can expand that valuable group by searching for "people who work at [insert company name] ..." By simply typing that term, you will receive another long list of people, with your first-degree connections at the top. You can also use the advanced search function and type IBM in the company name to get the same results. Again, those people listed first are going to be your most productive targets for informational meetings.

David Gafford's Information Meeting Journey

When I was looking for my next opportunity, I tried just about everything. I went to networking lunches for local business owners, I surfed LinkedIn and applied for jobs, I set up daily searches on Indeed and other job aggregators. It just didn't seem like anything was really moving the needle for me like I needed it to. My career coach suggested informational meetings with potential employers.

I saw the value in informational meetings immediately. Having the opportunity to sit down with someone from the company that I was considering working for and getting to hear their experiences? Priceless! What I didn't expect was how difficult it would be to get an initial meeting with people who had zero idea who I was. In the first round, my emails and LinkedIn requests looked something like this, "Dear (name), My name is David, and I would love to buy you coffee if you're up for it. I'm looking for my next career, and I would love to learn more about your company and why you love working there."

You can probably guess my success ratio with that email. I sent it out to about fifteen people, and I didn't get a single taker. I changed the email to this: "Dear (name), My name is David, and I would love to hear about your experiences with (company) and why you love working there. I'm seeking my next career, and I would love to hear your story about how you chose (company) and what makes (company) tick. Could I buy you a cup of coffee on your way to work and hear your story?"

Out of fifteen people that I sent that email to, two said yes. We were on our way now. During those meetings, I came with an arsenal of tools to help them remember me. I brought my resume, my cover letter, a folio of references, a thank you card, and business cards in case anything ever came up about me looking for a job. During those two meetings, I learned an incredibly valuable lesson. The meeting seemed to go really well when they talked about themselves and seemed to go poorly when we started to talk about me. When we talked about them, they were loose and enjoyed our time together. As soon as it shifted to me and looking for a job, they seemed to tense up, cross their arms, and send out other signals that this was getting uncomfortable.

So I rewrote my cold email to people I'd not yet met one final time. It read:

"Dear (name),
My name is David, and I would love to hear your story. I know you've been working with (company) for (X) years now, and I'm interested in learning more about your journey if you're up for it. Would you allow me to buy you coffee some morning on your way to work?

Full disclosure, I'm in a job transition, and I'm looking to learn more about what you do and your journey to where you are now. If you'd allow me to buy you a cup of coffee, here's what I promise.

1. I'll come to you. Wherever it's good for you to meet, I'll meet you there. If there's a coffee shop close to your office, just name the time and place and I'll be there.
2. I won't ask you for a job. I want to learn about you and your experiences and how I can apply them to where I go next.
3. I won't bring a resume or any job search materials.
4. I'll set a timer for fifteen minutes, and when the timer goes off, I'll head on my way. I know your time is valuable, and I want to honor that.
5. I'll buy the coffee.

I look forward to meeting you and learning more about your career. Have a wonderful day!

David"

Out of the next fifteen people that I sent my email to, can you guess how many took me up on the offer? <u>Thirteen out of the fifteen people I emailed took me up on the meeting</u>. It was a stunning turn of events in my job search.

During my fifteen minute meetings, I came armed with four primary questions:

1. Tell me about how you got started in (their current career).
2. Tell me about how you got started at (their current company).
3. What do you love about working at (their current company)?
4. If there was a piece of advice you could give to your former self five or ten years ago, what would it be?

For the rest of the meeting, I would always let their answers be my guide to follow-up questions.

Needless to say, I learned a lot from my experience with informational meetings. Among the most important discoveries:

1. People in authority positions don't feel appreciated very often. Many of the people I reached out to told me that they said yes to the meeting simply because I wanted to hear their story and talk to them! This point was incredibly important to the entire strategy. They met with me because <u>they felt good that I asked to hear their story</u>. The one thing I made sure of during each meeting was that they got to tell their story.

2. In almost every meeting, the person I was meeting with would tell me to turn off the timer before fifteen minutes was up. They were enjoying talking about themselves, and wanted to keep going. The average meeting for a fifteen minute coffee turned into about ninety minutes. Yes, you read that right. I asked for fifteen minutes, and they gave me ninety plus in most cases.

3. There is one thing that people love to talk about more than anything else in the world. Themselves. If you invite someone to talk about themselves, most people will gladly do so and will thoroughly enjoy it!

Dave's experience with informational meetings helped shape the idea that he had a lot of skills and capabilities on his own, and motivated him to start his own business. He successfully launched Fusion Creative, a digital marketing company helping business owners grow their traffic, their leads, and their sales. You can learn more about David and Fusion Creative at www.fusioncreative.org.

Since these people are first degree connections, you can send them "Inmails" through LinkedIn directly. Or, if you have an email address or phone number for them, you may prefer those, since not everyone is active on LinkedIn every day.

You aren't done yet, though. As you perform these searches you may find that you don't have any first-degree connections in the industry or company(ies), but will likely see someone listed as a second degree connection that you would like to meet. While non-premium (aka non-paying) LinkedIn members can't Inmail second degree connections, the reason they are listed as second degree is because they are first degree connections with one of your first-degree connections. They are sort of like a friend of a friend.

Using LinkedIn, you can very often get to that second-degree connection by leveraging your first-degree connection you have in common. Simply send a message to your first-degree connection asking for an introduction to the person you have in common. A message along these lines would be appropriate:

"Hey, Steve. I hope you are doing well at Oracle. I wonder if I could ask a favor. I am looking to make a job change and I am really interested in working for Gannett. I noticed that you are connected to Ted Drinkwater there. Would you mind introducing me to him? I'd love to sit down and pick his brain a bit. I really appreciate it."

Because of your connection to Steve (and the fact that what you are asking for is extremely easy for Steve to do), Steve is highly likely to make that introduction. (You may find situations, though, where Steve is connected to Ted, but they really don't know each other. In that case, Steve may not be comfortable making the introduction). Even better, since Steve is, in effect, referring you to Ted Drinkwater, Ted is much more likely to meet and help you because of that referral. Ted won't want to let Steve down!

Building Momentum

Years ago, there was a famous television commercial for Prell shampoo that, decades before the term "viral" was popular in social media, introduced the concept to advertising. In the ad campaign, a pretty young lady appeared on the screen extolling the virtues of Prell shampoo. In fact, she liked it so much that she "told two friends." When those words were spoken, her image was joined by two more images of herself. In unison, all three said that "they told two friends" at which time the number of images on the screen doubled.

This continued until, very soon, the screen was full of tiny images of the woman.

That campaign is almost fifty years old, having run in the 1970s. But the same principle still applies today, and it applies to informational meetings.

If your goal is to have eight informational meetings a week, you may have a fairly easy time getting eight people in your network to agree to meet. And you may find sixteen to fill up two weeks. But if you are like most people, at some point in the near future, you will exhaust your network. Then what?

Instead of simply "using up" your network, approach each informational meeting with the goal of securing two referrals to meet. By doing this, if all goes according to plan, after your first eight meetings, you will have sixteen more names to contact – with referrals! That fills up another two weeks! And if each of them gives you two more names, now you have thirty-two more. Your dance card is full for another four weeks! That's a heck of a lot easier than pouring over your network trying to find people you haven't met with yet.

You might notice I said if everything goes according to plan. Well, things never go according to plan all of the time. There will be people who do not give you any referrals. But there will be some that offer you three or more. And although you may not even average two per meeting, you will almost surely get enough to keep your calendar active and meet your weekly goal.

Final Notes on Informational Meetings

There is one very important activity that you MUST do after you have an informational meeting. You must follow up with a thank you note.

Some people prefer to send a thank you via email after a meeting and, if the person has requested a resume, this is a good time to attach it. Also, in certain companies and industries, email is the preferred method of communication, so sending the email version is completely acceptable.

On the other hand, again depending on the industry, a thank you card, handwritten and delivered by the U.S. Postal Service, is a very nice touch, and a memorable one. Nice cards often remain on the person's desk for a while and serve as a reminder of you and your job search.

Another "side-benefit" of informational meetings lies in meeting people inside the companies for which you want to work. As mentioned earlier, many companies now have referral programs where current employees can be paid from a few dollars to hundreds to even thousands of dollars for referring an applicant who gets hired. Employees that you meet through informational meetings are often very anxious to be an "inside" referral for you when jobs are posted. If you don't get hired, they aren't affected. But if you do get hired, they get paid!

I have heard time and time again from job seekers that, when they are frustrated and feeling as though they are just not making any progress in their search, holding an informational meeting gets them back on track emotionally. That may seem counterintuitive, but it is true. You may not feel like yet another meeting with yet another person you don't know, but, for whatever reason, it is a great pick me up!

Exercise: Networking to Find Employers

Step 1 – Make a list of key organizations you'd like to work for ("ultimate" companies)

Step 2 – List other competitors, peers

Step 3 – Document which industry they are in

Step 4 – Compile a list of target contacts from LinkedIn (and other sources) with whom you want an informational meeting

---

CHAPTER EIGHT

Marketing Yourself

By now you have probably gathered – and perhaps already experienced – that getting a new job can be a lot of work. Some even say that finding a job *is* a job! While that is certainly true, it is also very accurate to say, "Finding a job is really about selling yourself."

Unfortunately, most of us are uncomfortable selling ourselves. We are taught to be humble, not to toot our own horn, not to brag about our accomplishments. But if there is ever a time to "sell yourself," your job search is that time!

Who knows more about you and what you can do than you? How is someone going to discover the contributions you can make to their organization unless you tell them? The clearer and more often you communicate your message, the greater the chances of finding the right match for your talents, skills, and interests.

The Art of "Personal Branding"

When I say Coca-Cola, you know exactly what I am talking about. I don't have to explain that Coke is a caramel-colored, sugary soft drink. Your brain already knows that. If I say Progressive Insurance, you probably think of Flo, the spokesperson, or perhaps the fact that Progressive compares prices for you online. The words "dream car" may conjure up images of a Rolls Royce or Bentley in your mind.

Such reactions at the mention of these products is not because they are necessarily better than other products. Indeed, you may not have owned or used them (few of us have driven a Rolls Royce, but we certainly know what it is). Still, the mere mention stirs involuntary emotions within us. But product names like these go even further. With the mere mention of the product, we instinctively know the type of product it is, who is likely to buy and/or use it, and perhaps even experience deep feelings for it.

This, my friends, is the result of successful branding.

When you are looking for a product for your home, car, or personal care, how do you go about choosing that product? In many cases, it's due to the image you have of the company -- their brand. You may have past awareness and even experiences with the company, and are often familiar with slogans they have created to make that association in your mind. Do you recognize these brands?

"The ultimate driving machine" (BMW)
"Just do it" (Nike)
"Like a Good Neighbor" (State Farm Insurance)

These are word associations you recognize because these companies have spent literally millions of dollars to develop a theme and generate advertising around that theme – to target people that either currently need or will need their product. People like you. In addition, if you have used their product or service before, you have a perspective on its reputation, its value, as it were.

In your job search, branding is an important concept and one that, when executed well, can significantly shorten your search. A good personal brand will focus your search on those positions in which you want to work, plus it can make people within your network involuntarily think of you when they hear of the right opportunity.

Your personal brand is developed through careful thought and consideration in a way that can be concisely stated and carried across all the facets of your job search. Your resume should reflect your brand as well as your other supporting material.

"Personal" branding is about understanding and articulating:

- Who you are
- What you are good at (and best at!)
- Where you can best contribute
- How you add value to a prospective employer

The Building Blocks of Your Personal Brand

To "build your brand," you need to develop your most essential focus: What are your "Top things" (skills, strengths, experience) that <u>most translate to value</u> (to your target employer(s))? The key question to answer: what do you want someone to most remember about you, *five minutes after:*

- You have given your thirty second introduction, and walked away;
- They have put down your resume;
- They have viewed your LinkedIn profile?

Put yet another way: what concepts and words do you want your target audience – recruiters and prospective employers – to know about you? What word associations do you want to leave with them, that make them think of you when they consider the skills and strengths they need in the position? That's your brand!

For many job seekers, developing a concise and memorable brand can be quite difficult. We all inherently want to include everything about us rather than target our branding to a narrow focus. The temptation to offer everything to everyone so that we don't miss any potential opportunities usually results in a "shotgun" approach when a rifle is the much better choice.

Some of the most successful marketing has the simplest message. That's because our brains simply don't retain all that much information from the start! At most, we retain three to five key facts or concepts after an initial conversation. That's why it is critical to get across the very few key ideas you want to leave with your reader or listener. Does Subaru make cars that may appeal to many different tastes? Sure. But its branding is all about safety. It doesn't try to be everything to everyone. Can you get top-end tools and hardware at Menards? You bet. But their brand is "Save Big Money."

The most effective use of your time, energy, and resources in branding is to choose a target and focus on it like a laser. You may have lots of other skills, but trying to promote everything you can do to everyone simply spreads your message too thin, may make you look desperate or overqualified, and will probably dramatically lengthen your job search.

The Business Card

The business card has been around for generations and you surely used one in your last position, handing it out to others as a reminder of meetings or to provide contact information for later use. Now that you are looking for a new job, you probably don't have a business card. But you should!

The business card is not just a piece of cardstock to give colleagues and enter contests to win free lunches. As a job seeker, your business card will serve other extremely important purposes. Your business card will be a mini-resume, used to inform others about you and your capabilities as well as to plant the seeds of your personal brand.

The typical business card has very little information beyond a name, title, company name, address, phone number, and probably an email address. A company logo is often used (which, by the way, is part of the branding effort of the company). A job seeker's business card has much more.

Your new business card will use both sides of the card and contain the traditional information such as:

- Your name
- Your phone number

- Your email address
- The job title and/or industry you are pursuing

But, unlike many traditional cards, the back of your business card will contain your "mini-resume."

You may have struggled to fit your resume on two pages (or one!). How in the world can you put your resume on a business card? You can't. But you can put the highlights on your business card that are most likely to draw attention and, of course, to develop your brand.

If you are a chief financial officer, that title would go on the front of your card. On the back, a list of no more than five or six of your accomplishments, bulleted, short, and easy to read. Perhaps you managed a $100M budget. "Managed $100M budgets" is a great bullet point. Did you cut benefit costs by 5%? "Benefit cost control" would be good on the back of the card. Where you able to restructure capital to reduce taxes for the company by 15%? "Tax Management" is another item to include.

Each of the items that you choose to include on your mini-resume must correspond to the brand you are trying to develop. What if you also served on a committee that chose a new software program for HR? Great. But that has nothing to do with your being an excellent CFO. Talk about that in an interview if it's appropriate, but leave it off the card.

An excellent source for the bullet points to include on the back of your job search business card is to review your strengths that you developed through the exercises in Chapter 5.

Beyond the basic contact information and your mini-resume on the back, there are really no limits to the design of your card. I've included a couple for your review.

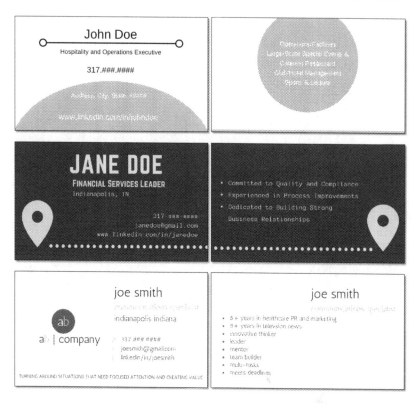

Once you have designed and ordered your job search business cards and have them in hand, you will probably wonder what exactly to do with them.

Networking is more than just meeting people and telling them you need a job. And handing a resume to everyone you know will not only turn them off (as they will think you are trying to apply for a job with them) but, since the way to a job is to customize your resume to the position, giving your contact a generic version may not have the intended impact.

The first effective step in networking is to offer your job search business card whenever you meet someone. However, don't offer it like most people offer a business card. Always offer yours face DOWN. Why? Because this assures the recipient will see your mini-resume first. People will always turn it over to see your name and contact information. But if you hand it to someone face up, they may never think to look at the back where all the important information about you and your brand reside.

The Marketing Profile

Chances are you will conduct lots of informational meetings in your quest for your next job. You may have met some of these people previously – in which case you probably gave them a business card – or this may be the first time you are meeting face-to-face. In that case, be sure to offer your job search business card (face down!) upon meeting. There is a second technique you should use whenever you hold a face-to-face informational meeting. At our Team Networking Group, we call it a marketing profile.

When you meet someone in person, you should offer them your marketing profile. This is a one-page sheet, using front and back if needed, which provides both visual interest and information not found in your resume. It is, in effect, a less-threatening way to introduce yourself professionally than handing out resumes.

Later in this chapter is an exercise you can use to design your own marketing profile. A template is also included in the appendix. But you should know that you should strive to make your marketing profile unique. In other words, use the template to help create your brand! No two are exactly alike and they shouldn't be!

The example and template are very basic. That is done on purpose. This will provide a starting point for you, but I hope you embellish it to make it your own. Unlike on your resume, this is a great time to experiment with color and patterns. An eye-catching border may help it stand out. Experiment with different fonts and colors. Some people orient their marketing profile in portrait (like this book) while others prefer landscape. There is no right answer. It is completely up to you.

The Marketing Profile is a "Fact Sheet" about you, adapting <u>key content</u> from your resume and distilling it to one page. It is high-level, visually pleasing, easy to read, and understandable. It's far more informal than a resume, and because it's a different format, it catches people's attention – from recruiters, to your informational meeting audience, even to HR professionals in the interviewing process.

Format

Here are the key sections of your Marketing Profile:

<u>Name, Contact Information, and Target Role/Area</u>

- This section of your Marketing Profile should be similar to your LinkedIn headline: short, simple – communicates what you are looking for.

<u>Picture</u>

- Include a "headshot" picture of yourself – it has to look good, though you don't have to pay a professional photographer with the level of technology available today. Easiest: use a copy of the photo you have on your LinkedIn profile.

<u>Who I Am</u>

- Brief narrative summary (about three sentences, summarizing who you are professionally.)

<u>What I Provide</u>

- Key skills, capabilities, personal strengths, and attributes you bring.

<u>What I've Done</u>

- Key Accomplishments (three to four STAR Stories that represent you *at your best*, that apply to your target position – with results!)

How I Add Value

- What is a pattern of results/success that is typical of your work?
- How will you <u>contribute the most</u> to your target organization?

Target Role / Area / Group

- Name the functional job titles you are targeting
- Include target industries you want
- Also, you can include target areas (e.g. Operations, or Financial Management)
- Optional: Some people like to put specific organizations or companies of interest. This may be helpful – or it may send a mixed signal if you are speaking with someone at Company A and you also have a direct competitor's name on the list. It's up to you how to play this. Prompting someone with a specific company may help them think of contacts for you. But it might also give the impression that you aren't interested in other companies.

Desired Contacts

- At what level or functional roles are the kinds of people you are most interested in speaking with? (e.g., Finance/Accounting – would probably be CFO or Controller)

Example

Here's a sample view of a marketing profile:

Susan Seeker
Operations Management
Indianapolis, IN   317-555-5555
Susan.career.seeker@gmail.com
https://www.linkedin.com/in/susancareerseeker

Who I Am:
Creative, hands-on business leader with 15+ years' experience with Fortune 500 firms spanning product management, CRM, and delivery operations. Focused on innovation, customer service, and business process improvement through results-driven project management and operational excellence.

What I Provide:
- Strategy, Process improvement, CQI
- Data analysis
- Financial analysis
- Resource/capacity demand
- CRM and Portfolio management
- Lean Six Sigma – GreenBelt
- Microsoft Office, Project, SharePoint
- SAP JMP, SAP/Business Warehouse

What I've Done:
- Successfully managed process change, contingency plans, cost/benefit analysis to increase business performance and productivity, within budget.

- Managed diverse, multidisciplinary, and multi-site teams to promote sustainable change.
- Formulated policies, streamlined sales processes, and anticipated industry and market trends to create strategies and identify viable business growth opportunities.
- Implemented process improvements that reduced customer complaints by 60%, with a savings of $18,000-$20,000 annually.
- Developed a strong team of 20 Service Providers through training, mentoring, follow-up, and accountability.

How I Add Value:
- Actively seek out opportunities to strengthen and exceed operational goals and objectives.
- Systematic with "big picture" vision, to convert complex requirements into actionable projects and plans.
- Deliver outstanding customer relationship management and retention strategies.
- Build strong teams by cultivating trust, instilling confidence, and collaborating with leaders, customers, stakeholders, and subject matter experts.

Target Positions:
- Operations Manager
- Operations Consultant
- Senior Business Analyst
- Project Manager

Target Companies/Industries:
- Companies focused on superior customer service and fulfillment, who value customers and employees
- Healthcare/Life Sciences
- Biotechnology
- Pharmaceutical
- Energy and Environmental
- Insurance

Desired Contacts:
- COO, Director of Operations
- Vice President/Regional Executive
- HR Executive

Sometimes job seekers resist using Marketing Profiles. After all, they likely haven't seen one used before. And that's the point! The Marketing Profile allows you to appear different than other job seekers and in a professional way.

Advantages of using a Marketing Profile include:

- Informality – It doesn't look or feel like a resume, because it's really not.
- Creativity – This is a different take, and not familiar to most people. It will help you stand out in a positive way and be remembered as unique.
- Brevity – It's concise, especially when so many resumes ramble on to multiple pages. Thomas Jefferson once said, *"The most valuable of all talents is that of never using two words when one will do."*
- Consistency – The key message must be consistent with your resume and LinkedIn profile.
- Effective – It gets your key message across!
- Portability – Have a printed copy with you. Also, save it as a PDF document – you can easily share it via email as a follow-up to informational meetings.
- Utility – You can use it in various networking formats, including follow-up with contacts you meet at networking events or career fairs, your "network newsletter" (see Chapter 12), informational meetings, or as a follow-up to informational meetings. You can even include a copy in the information packet you take to a formal job interview. We have heard great stories of Human Resources professionals who were

intrigued by this format and gave a positive impression to hiring managers after seeing this along with a resume.

Exercise:

You're likely great at something! But, does your Marketing Profile highlight it? Does your resume reflect it? How about your LinkedIn profile? Do they reflect your brand, your focus? As you work through this process:

- Condense, distill: What are your *Top three to five* Strengths or Personal Attributes, Soft (Transferable) Skills, Hard (Specific Domain/Industry/Knowledge) Skills?
- Work toward key words and phrases.
- Draft your one-page Marketing Profile.
- Write, rewrite, rewrite again. This takes time and reflection. Share it with those in your support network for their feedback.

Now, take it along with you to your next informational meeting. At the close, if you have a good rapport with the person, you can ask, "I have a personal 'fact sheet' that helps describe my capabilities. Would that be of interest to you?" If they are agreeable, give them a copy. Or, if the timing doesn't feel right, keep it for now. It may be that after your meeting and the follow-up email thank-you, it will be appropriate to include as a soft-copy.

As you use this, you will probably edit, tweak, and adjust it. Perfect! That too is part of the journey. "Marketing" yourself may sound forced or artificial to you. By contrast, marketing is essentially just telling a story. This is a way to help you tell your own story.

Most importantly, have fun with it!

30-Second Introduction

Another key component in your branding is the 30-second introduction. This goes by many names, including the "elevator speech," the "30-second commercial," and even your "30-second infomercial."

Have you ever been watching television when you come across one of those half-hour commercials that you just can't help watching? You know you probably aren't going to buy a new knife that cuts cans and bricks and still cuts tomatoes. You aren't in the market for a countertop rotisserie. Yet there you are, watching intently, until someone else comes into the room and you switch channels quickly to give the impression that you were just passing it while changing channels.

The fact is, those half-hour commercials, known as infomercials, are masters of branding. How can you forget a knife that cuts cans? That slogan for the rotisserie ("Set It and Forget It!") is stuck in your head for hours.

In most cases, you don't have thirty minutes to explain who you are and what you want to do. But you do have thirty seconds. So you need to be ready.

The "30-Second Introduction" is your opportunity to softly market yourself, in a verbal introduction, where, in addition to giving your name, you provide your skill sets that make great first impressions to prospective employers. This can be used during a job interview, during an elevator ride, or when talking with a potential network resource.

Your "30-Second Introduction" is YOU: it is what YOU do and where you want to go. Opportunities occur when an employer or networker asks, "Tell me about yourself." YOU must be ready to take charge of that discussion as it must become second nature when those opportunities occur.

Outline of a 30-Second Introduction

1. Who are you?

- Name

2. What job(s) do you seek?

- Job Titles/Areas of the Company

3. What are your strengths?

- Briefly outline three of your key strengths/skills

4. What benefits/value do you bring?

- Give one-two brief examples
- "Sell yourself" (brag just a little!) – tell how good you are

5. Where do you want to work?

- List ideal job(s), ideal companies

6. Close with your name

7. Who do you know that I might speak with?

All this information may seem like a lot to pack into thirty seconds, but it can be done quite easily. Later in the chapter, I will give you a template to build your own thirty second infomercial.

Including the points mentioned above is crucial, as it serves two purposes. First, it relates your brand, succinctly stating who you are and what you do. Second, it focuses the person listening in such a way as to make it more likely that they will help you.

If I were to ask you to name five people you know, you could surely perform that request quickly and easily. However, if I were a job seeker and looking to network in a target company or two, a random list of names is not going to be very helpful. If I asked you to think of five people who like sports, you may or may not be able to do that on the spot. Most people could only name two or three. But if I asked you to name the people on the team in your Sunday afternoon basketball league, you could rattle off those names easily! The same logic applies to the thirty second infomercial.

Too often, job seekers simply ask others if they know of anyone looking to hire or if they know of any openings. That request is much too broad and will likely yield few results and those that it does provide will probably not be what you are looking for. Instead, by using the structure of the thirty second infomercial, you are subconsciously steering the listener's thought process to places where it is easier to recall potential contacts and positions.

If you are in construction, telling someone you know that you are looking for a new job in the industry would most likely result in an answer like, "Well, I don't know anyone but I'll keep my eyes open." But by telling the other person (in your thirty second infomercial) that you have worked on several home remodeling projects and asking if they know anyone who is doing good work like that in the area, the other person is much more likely to think of the company that remodeled his kitchen a few years ago. Or to think of the company that built the addition to the home next door.

Networking is not just about finding job openings. After all, most job openings are not made public. It is about making connections that can lead you to job openings. An effective job seeker doesn't ask if the person knows of any jobs. An effective job seeker asks for connections in the companies and industries where he or she wants to work. That's the goal of the thirty second infomercial.

Take a few minutes to build your thirty second infomercial using this template. Then commit it to memory and try it out on some of your contacts. Don't be surprised when you feel the need to revise it. It will evolve over time, believe me.

Exercise:

Hello, my name is [insert name]. I am a [job title], who just finished an engagement and am looking for my next position. I am a [key strength], [key strength], and [key strength], and even [success example], [success example], and [success example].

I am very interested in working as a [title or role] with [target company] or [target company].

Again, my name is [insert name]. Do you happen to know anyone I should talk to?

It is natural for job seekers to gain confidence in themselves as they work through the process of branding and job searching. Developing your Marketing Profile helps get your brand, your message, concise -- down to a single page. Crafting and practicing a brief introduction of yourself in about thirty seconds helps crystalize it to a few key points.

To summarize what to use when, carry your job search business cards with you at all times and whenever you meet someone new, provide one of those cards – face down. Whenever you meet someone for an informational meeting, be sure to bring along a couple copies of your Marketing Profile. Only when you are in a formal job interview, provide your resume.

CHAPTER NINE
LinkedIn

The authors would like to thank Julie Bondy Roberts for her contributions to this chapter. For more information about Julie and her "badass" LinkedIn profiles, visit her on LinkedIn at www. linkedin.com/in/juliebondyroberts/.

Overheard at a networking event for job searchers:

Job Searcher #1: I don't use that LinkedIn thing.

Job Searcher #2: And you don't have a job!

It has been shown time and time again that networking is very often the key to finding not just a job, but a great job. There's only one problem. Most of us hate networking. Furthermore, most of us aren't terribly good at it.

Going to a meeting at some restaurant with twenty-five to thirty people you don't know, making small talk, trying to break into conversations and escape unproductive ones, all the while just hoping someone there knows of a job for you, is tiring, tedious, and, frankly, nothing anyone really anticipates.

But imagine if you could network with literally millions of people, easily identify those in your industry or currently working at your target companies, and even directly interact with HR professionals, all without leaving your home!

You don't have to imagine it. It already exists!

It's called LinkedIn.

While that local networking meeting might be full of small business people, sales people, and other job seekers, you may not have much luck finding some vice president seeking your skill set to offer you a job.

LinkedIn, on the other hand, is a community of over 500,000,000 business people,[18] 133,000,000 of which are located in the United States, and every one of them is accessible to you. Every month, over 106,000,000 members are active on the site and 40% use LinkedIn every day! And, if the person you are trying to find isn't on there, just wait; LinkedIn adds two new members every SECOND.

Of all those people using LinkedIn, consider these facts:

- 44% of LinkedIn users earn more than $75,000 per year.
- 41% of millionaires use LinkedIn.
- The average user spends seventeen minutes each month on LinkedIn.

In 2016, Microsoft saw the incredible potential in the LinkedIn community and purchased it for $26.2 billion! Most important to a job seeker, LinkedIn averages 3,000,000 job listings at any given time![19]

---

[18] Darrow, Barb, "LinkedIn Claims Half a Billion Users," fortune.com/2017/04/24/linkedin-users/, April 24, 2017, Web, November 17, 2017.

[19] Chaudhary, Meenakshi, "LinkedIn By The Numbers: 2017 Statistics," www.linkedin.com/pulse/linkedin-numbers-2017-statistics-meenakshi-chaudhary, LinkedIn.com, April 5, 2017, Web, November 17, 2017.

Recruiters and LinkedIn

The website Jobvite conducts an annual survey on recruiting and social media, the most extensive survey in the recruiting industry. The 2015 version reported that 94% of recruiters use LinkedIn to source candidates. While Facebook has more users, only 66% of recruiters reported use Facebook to find candidates.[20] (This makes sense, as Facebook is much more for social interaction, whereas LinkedIn is devoted to business). 19% of the recruiters reported finding better candidates through LinkedIn and social networking than through other means like job boards and company website postings.[21]

LinkedIn averages 3,000,000 job listing at any given time.

However, given that many active users and that much daily activity, the trick to using LinkedIn successfully in your job search boils down to two things: first, make it as easy as possible to be found, and second, give the recruiter something to like when they do find you!

LinkedIn Algorithms

There is no group of people sitting at the LinkedIn headquarters physically connecting job seekers. It is all done by computer algorithms (formulae) that try to make the computers find the right results and display them to the appropriate person. Those algorithms are the key to LinkedIn (and any technology-based company) and are not public knowledge. On top of that, they change them frequently in

[20] "Jobvite's New 2015 Recruiter Nation Survey Reveals Talent Crunch," www.jobvite.com/news item/jobvites-new-2015-recruiter-nation-survey-reveals-talent-crunch-95-recruiters-anticipate-similar-increased-competition-skilled-workers-coming-year-86-expect-exp/, September 22, 2015, Web, November 17, 2017.
[21] Weiss, Alyson, "The State of Social Recruiting in 2015," www.careermovesjvs.blogspot.com/2014/10/the-state-of-social-recruiting-in-2015.html, careermovesjvs.blogspot.com, October 15, 2014, Web, November 17, 2017.

a constant effort to improve the results. So, in reality, something in your profile that makes you stand out to recruiters today may not work tomorrow. Worst of all, you may not know why.

However, there are some basics that contribute to the likelihood of your job search success on LinkedIn that are highly unlikely to change.

All Star Status

LinkedIn assigns a rating to all profiles, termed "Profile Strength." There are five categories for profile strengths:

1. Beginner
2. Intermediate
3. Advanced
4. Expert
5. All Star

The goal of every job seeker should be All Star. The reason is quite simple. According to the online job seeker website, The Muse, those with All Star profiles are forty times more likely to receive opportunities through LinkedIn than those with lesser profile strengths. And, luckily for you, only about half of the profiles on LinkedIn are complete enough to achieve All Star status.[22] LinkedIn's algorithms "prefer" complete profiles. Those with complete profiles land higher in a recruiter's search results. Those with incomplete profiles land at the bottom.

Unlike many of the "secrets" of LinkedIn, the requirements to achieve that coveted All Star status are well known.

---

[22] Tanner, Nathan, "All-Star LinkedIn Users Are 40 Times More Likely to Get Contacted – Here's How to Score That Rating," www.themuse.com/advice/allstar-linkedin-users-are-40-times-more-likely-to-get-contactedheres-how-to-score-that-rating, Publication Date Unknown, Web, November 17, 2017.

1. *Profile photo*

   Although you may value your anonymity, when you are relying on the LinkedIn community to help you in your job search, that is no time to hide. LinkedIn users who encounter a profile without a photo often assume the profile is at least incomplete (and, thus, not accurate), or at most, dormant (meaning someone started setting it up then just didn't do anything more with it). Not having a profile picture sends the message that you have something to hide ... or worse! According to LinkedIn itself, by simply adding a profile picture you are seven times more likely to be found when searches are conducted.

   There is an art to choosing a profile picture for LinkedIn. Above all, it should be a professional photo. This doesn't necessarily mean that it has to be done by a professional photographer (although that is preferable). It simply means it should be a good, clear headshot of you in appropriate attire for the job you are doing or pursuing. Save the pictures of you with your family, the pets, rooting for your college football team, or at Mardi Gras for Facebook.

2. *An industry and location*

   LinkedIn allows you to select the industry you are in when creating (or updating) your profile. It also requests that you choose a location, usually an "area" near a large city such as "Chicago, Illinois area," or "San Francisco, California area." LinkedIn's algorithms will not grant All Star status without an industry and location.

   If, as a job seeker, you are interested in changing industries, consider changing your industry to the one you are looking for. That way, when recruiters and others filter by industry, your name will come up in those you want rather than the one(s) you are currently in or have been in previously. The same holds true for location.

3. *Education*

LinkedIn also requires an education history for All Star status. Be sure to include schools you attended. There is no requirement that you graduated, so include any and all schools that you attended – or are currently attending.

4. *A current position*

This is the one requirement for All Star status that trips up most job seekers. When a person leaves a position, voluntarily or otherwise, the first inclination is to change current position to something like "unemployed," or "seeking new opportunities," or, worst of all, to leave it blank. Unfortunately, LinkedIn algorithms will take away your All Star status if you do so.

There is a true split among career coaches as to whether you should say you are unemployed or looking on LinkedIn. Many say that this turns off recruiters who would much rather find candidates that are currently working. They argue that the stigma of being out of work is still present. However, there are many people who have listed their current status as unemployed who found jobs quickly. LinkedIn Guru and Career Coach Julie Bondy Roberts firmly believes that job seekers should avoid putting "unemployed," "looking for a new opportunity," or anything similar on a LinkedIn profile. According to Julie, putting "unemployed" or "seeking employment" in your headline causes two unintended consequences: 1) You put the focus on YOU rather than on what an employer needs. The most desirable candidates make their value to a future employer clear. 2) "Unemployed" and "Seeking Employment" are a waste of prime real estate;

they are not words that recruiters would ever use to find you. Instead, you should use words that convey your brand and value. The current position field actually presents an opportunity for job seekers. Many, many job seekers list their current position in terms of what they are looking for, or as a consultant to the industry in which they want to work. While it may feel a bit strange at first to call yourself a consultant when you aren't doing any consulting work, this is a proper strategy to employ. A doctor who is just starting his practice and doesn't have any patients yet is still a doctor! A builder who is between projects is still a builder! When you list yourself as a consultant, then, when someone searches in the industry, you will appear in the results.

5. *Past positions*

While you may be interested in distancing yourself from your past or current position, especially if you are interested in changing careers, LinkedIn will only award you All Star strength if you include at least two past positions. These can be with the same company or different companies.

This is also an opportunity for you to explain what you did in each position, including skills and experience that are transferable to a new position or career.

6. *Skills*

When creating a LinkedIn profile, you are able to select skills to be listed in your profile. All Star status requires at least three, although most people have many more (LinkedIn allows you to list up to fifty). You should be careful to select only those skills which you have, and make sure not to include too many. Someone with dozens and dozens of skills often looks suspicious to others, not to mention arrogant.

A good tip for job seekers when it comes to skills is to choose your top ten, preferably in order of importance, then send a message to people in your network letting them know that you have made revisions to your profile and would appreciate it if they would endorse you for those skills. Immediately, you can build credibility for your skills by increasing the number of endorsements!

7. *Connections*

There are two important numbers in LinkedIn when it comes to connections. The first is fifty. Fifty connections are required for All Star strength. However, the second number is even more important: 500. Good things happen in LinkedIn to those with at least 500 connections. More on that later in the chapter.

Being Found in Searches

LinkedIn is, at its heart, a giant database of information. LinkedIn's beauty lies in the fact that it is searchable on numerous levels. To make the most of this giant database, you must do what you can to be found. This is known as profile optimization. Optimizing your profile is the number one thing you can do to be found by recruiters and others and, ultimately, to land the job you want.

Although no one outside of LinkedIn knows for certain how the search function works, specific elements of your profile do impact the search results. Probably the most important is the headline.

Headline

The headline appears right next to your picture when anyone looks at your profile. LinkedIn allows up to 120 characters in your headline. These 120 characters are the most important in your entire profile in terms of searching. Using keywords that are appropriate for your career is crucial. In addition, being creative enough to make someone want to read your profile after you are found is just as important.

The majority of people on LinkedIn simply list their job title and company name as their headline. "Industrial Engineer," or "Project Manager," while descriptive and accurate, do nothing to make your profile unique. Plus, using only ten or fifteen characters in your headline leaves lots of characters "on the table" that may be useful in both describing your value and making sure others find you and read on.

Consider these headlines:

- Director of Engineering | Strategic Technology Planning | Develops High-Performing Engineering Teams | Delivers Results

- Saving $$ with Smart Process Improvements | Operations Management: Food Service, Facilities, Catering, P&L | Team Builder

- Customer Focused, Revenue & Profit Driven Omni-Channel Executive | Turnaround Strategist | Scalable Growth Strategy

- Program Management | Lifecycle Project Management | Process Improvement | Agile Methodologies | 317.553.5433

- Leads Operational Excellence & Bottom Line Growth Initiatives | Senior Operations Leader | Strategic Planner

---

Use your headline to your advantage. Save your job title for the "position title" field.

Summary

The "meat" of your LinkedIn profile is the summary. LinkedIn allows up to 2,000 characters, though most people use much less. The summary section is a large canvas on which to paint your story, from what you have done, to what you can do, to what you want to do. The typical summary is generally a recitation of the person's resume. But, as a job seeker, use this opportunity to make it much more. Your LinkedIn summary should be, first and foremost, conversational. It should be easy to read and tell the story of your "brand."

The summary is also prime real estate for keywords. This, like the headline, is one of the most searchable fields on LinkedIn. So make sure that you use those keywords appropriate to your industry and desired position prominently and often!

A great way to know the keywords you should include in the summary is to read job descriptions for your target job. The more a word is mentioned in the job description, the more important it is. Consequently, the more often a recruiter will likely search for that keyword.

Another great tip is to use a word cloud. Word clouds present visual representations of words in a document, making the most important words larger and the less important ones smaller. There are several free websites that will create word clouds for you. (You can see an example of a word cloud as well as instructions on creating one in Chapter 11.) The words that appear largest in a word cloud are likely the keywords for the job you are seeking. So be sure to pepper your summary with those words!

Endorsements and Recommendations

LinkedIn allows both recommendations and endorsements. Endorsements are more common, as they just require a click of a button. For example, if you have listed sales as a skill, a click of the "+" icon next to the skill by one of your connections increases the count for that skill by one. Typically, people looking at your skills assume that the ones with the highest numbers are the ones in which you are most proficient. If a recruiter is searching for a human resources generalist, the fact that you have lots of endorsements for human resources would likely be a good sign to that recruiter. LinkedIn shows the number of endorsements one-by-one until you hit ninety-nine. After that, the number does not change and is simply listed as "99+."

Julie Bondy Roberts offers a more in-depth take on endorsements. She believes endorsements are a lightning rod for heated debate because it's easy to endorse people in your network with just a click, whether you've witnessed that skill or not. That said, LinkedIn indicates that the more endorsements you have, the higher up you appear in a search result. At the very least, ask your colleagues who know you to endorse you, and return the favor.

Be career-savvy and manage this part of your LinkedIn Profile. Review your skills and endorsements tapestry every six to twelve months to make sure they represent you accurately. For example, if you used to be in charge of omni-channel marketing and your interests and experience is shifting to program development, update your endorsements section to reflect that.

Recommendations are rarer and, arguably, more valuable. A recommendation comes from someone who actually writes about you and the good work you do. A recommendation is, therefore, much more of a commitment than an endorsement.

When someone writes a recommendation for you, you will receive a notification before it is posted. While you cannot change someone's recommendation of you, you can elect not to show it on your profile or opt to ask the person for changes before it is posted. Some savvy LinkedIn users request recommendations from others and even provide a template to follow to make the recommendation easier. Be careful though. If you have ten recommendations, and they all follow the same format, it will be apparent what is going on!

<u>Your Contact Information</u>

While LinkedIn offers the opportunity to send messages, like private LinkedIn emails, among connections, job seekers should strongly consider including contact information in their profile. This is a good idea for a couple reasons. First, to contact you using LinkedIn messaging, the other person must be a premium member or a contact of yours (More on premium later in the chapter). If you include your email and/or a phone number, anyone who sees your profile can contact you. Second, listing ways to contact you allows you to include a call to action in your summary. Encourage others to reach out with a statement such as, "If you are interested in working with the best process improvement specialist in Texas, give me a call!" A call to action increases the chances that someone will reach out to you, potentially with an opportunity.

Letting Recruiters Know You Are Available

There is also a setting in LinkedIn that makes your profile available for viewing by recruiters without allowing others to know you are job searching. This is ideal when you are looking for a new position but are still working at another. It is called, "Open Candidates." To signal recruiters that you are open to a new opportunity, open the "preferences" tab on the LinkedIn Jobs page. Turn sharing "on" and complete some information about the types of jobs you are interested in. That's it!

You might wonder how a recruiter can see that you are looking but others can't. Recruiters have a special membership to LinkedIn which is quite pricey. Through this special membership they can view things that others cannot. So they will get the "signal" but no one else will. And, relax. Even if your company has the recruiter subscription, LinkedIn will hide your profile from your company and any affiliated companies.

500+ Connections

Earlier I mentioned that having 500 or more connections is the goal for a job seeker. While that may seem rather daunting, it is very doable and has some significant benefits.

First is credibility in the LinkedIn community. Those familiar with LinkedIn automatically recognize that you are connected and active when you have the magic 500+ moniker on your profile.

Second, the more connections you have, the more you appear in search results. This is because search results favor people you are connected to. Put another way, if you are directly connected to someone who searches for your job title, you will come up at or near the top of the list. Similarly, if you are a second-degree connection of someone (that is, you are connected to someone who is connected to the person), you will still appear in the search, although not necessarily at the very top. Even third-degree connections will get some preference when it comes to search results as compared to those people to whom you have no connection.

Let's say you are interested in a job with ABC Corporation, a mid-sized business in your town. LinkedIn allows you to search for employees at that company.

For illustration purposes, if you have fifty connections, each of whom has fifty connections, you have fifty first degree connections, and 2,500 second degree connections. If you search for ABC Corporation, those first and second-degree connections will show up first. In a relatively small group like that, you may or may not find what you are looking for.

On the other hand, if you have 200 connections and so do your 200 connections, in addition to having 200 first degree connections, you now have 40,000 second degree connections. The chances that your search will be successful just increased by sixteen times!

If you are at the magic 500 number and so are your connections, your 500 first degrees will connect you to 250,000 other people! Surely you will be successful in finding what you are looking for now. That's an increase of 100 times over having fifty connections!

Follow Your Target Companies

It is also a good idea to "follow" companies you are interested in. This can be done by visiting the company's LinkedIn page and clicking the "follow" button. By following a company, you will begin receiving any updates the company posts. Many companies also post their current job openings on LinkedIn, and you will receive the notification first. Plus, by following the company, you will get valuable information about the activities at the firm that you can use in your interview preparation.

Can LinkedIn really lead to a new job?

These are reports from two real job seekers who believe it can:

"At first, I was hesitant to believe that LinkedIn could do anything that I could not do on my own, but after optimizing my LinkedIn profile, I was able to turn my small investment in a LinkedIn coach into an incredible profit -- a job offer fifteen times my investment, within twenty-four hours of going live." - Drew

"Immediately after optimizing my LinkedIn profile, I saw results. Not only have my profile views jumped substantially, but I was contacted by a former colleague about a new position. It worked for me!" - Terry

---

Posting Updates on Your Job Search

Some job seekers use LinkedIn to post updates on the job search process. This can be a mixed bag, of course, and something you wouldn't want to do if you are still employed elsewhere. Some people believe posting job search updates not only alerts others that you are out of work (there's that stigma again), but can also make you appear somewhat desperate. Others, however, find that their network can be very helpful in finding a new position.

The key to posting job search updates on LinkedIn is to sound upbeat while simultaneously mentioning target goals. For example, rather than posting, "I am looking for a job after ten years at IBM.

If you know of any leads, please let me know," try something like, "I recently learned that BetterCross, Inc., is looking for an executive assistant! I would love to work there. Does anyone have any advice?" This post invites others to help and mentions a company. More than likely, this will result in others in your network letting you know of connections they have at BetterCross, Inc. (Although we are talking about LinkedIn, this strategy can also be very successful on Facebook and other social networking sites).

Being Active on LinkedIn

The key to posting job search updates on LinkedIn is to appear upbeat while at the same time mentioning targeting goals.

Unfortunately, just having a great profile and lots of connections is not enough. To increase your chances of being found – and of your dream job finding you – you also need to be active on LinkedIn on a regular basis. Like many other strategies, there are multiple ways to do it. They include:

- Regular posting of status updates including links and articles;
- Publishing posts relevant to your industry;
- Joining and being active in groups;
- Generously "tagging" others.

The thought of regularly posting new content on LinkedIn is scary for most people. They can't think of anything to say or are afraid to create controversy. But regularly posting an update is a key to increasing your visibility and, hopefully, landing that new role.

An easy way to approach this strategy is by using something called "Google Alerts." Simply search Google for Google Alerts and you will find instructions on creating a Google Alert. By choosing a topic (or two or three) that is pertinent to your industry or job search and choosing how often you would like to receive the alerts (daily, weekly, etc.), Google will scour the internet for any new information on the topic you have chosen. You will get an email at the chosen interval with links to articles from various sources on the topic. Then you can simply post the link as a LinkedIn update (preferably with a little introduction from yourself such as, "Great article on the future of Learning and Development"). Job done! People will read the article, may react to it with a "like" or a comment, and, most likely, some will want to connect with you. And if someone disagrees, they aren't disagreeing with you, but with the author of the article.

One of the most powerful "tricks" to use when posting status updates on LinkedIn is to tag others, especially those in your network. Whenever you post a new update or reply to someone else's update, whenever possible, mention someone in your network by name. When you want to tag someone in your post, type the "@" symbol followed immediately by the person's name. As you begin typing the name, LinkedIn will show you the names of your connections that match. Select the one you want and that name will be included in your response. Even better, your post or reply will then show up in the feeds of all of that person's connections! Consider that for a second. Even if you only had ten connections, if you mention a first-degree connection with 1,000 connections, your post goes not just to your ten, but to her 1,000! And if one of them reposts it or tags someone else in a reply, it keeps going!

LinkedIn also allows you to write and publish articles that are then made available not only to your connections but to anyone on LinkedIn to read. These do not need to be in-depth or lengthy; in fact, most are not much longer than one page. If readers like what they see, based on activity, it may be promoted to others outside of your network. This can result in increasing your credibility in the industry as well as encouraging others to connect with you.

From the LinkedIn homepage, you will see the option to publish a post. Choose a topic that is relevant and timely in the industry you want to work and write away. One tip: posts with a picture are read more often than those without!

Making LinkedIn Work for You

Thus far, we have looked at LinkedIn in a reactive way. You are trying to be found and contacted by others. But you also need to be proactive.

LinkedIn has a very robust search engine allowing you to search for just about any company, job, and person by name. For a job seeker, one of the most powerful searches is simply for "people who work at XYZ." This search will return everyone on LinkedIn who works or has worked for XYZ. Of course, your first-degree connections will be first, your second-degree connections next, etc. As illustrated earlier, the larger your network, the more likely you will find someone at XYZ in your network to whom you can reach out for an information meeting (see Chapter 7). And, assuming you received too many results to be helpful, LinkedIn offers filters on the search engine to limit the results to just people in a given area, with a certain title, or those currently work at XYZ.

There is no better way to find people who can help you in your job search than the LinkedIn search engine.

LinkedIn also offers another free benefit to job seekers: the LinkedIn Job Search App.

This app is available for Android and Apple smartphones and is a great tool for getting the latest job posting on LinkedIn. You can set up alerts, save jobs you want to apply to, see similar jobs from other companies, and even apply to some positions right from your phone using your LinkedIn profile. My experience is that I often see jobs on the LinkedIn Job Search App that I have not seen posted elsewhere.

As a final note to this very cursory look at the way LinkedIn works, you will no doubt receive solicitations and suggestions from LinkedIn that you should become a premium member. The advertisements will make it sound as if you can't be successful without it. But before you incur another expense, here are some things you should consider.

1. *It's expensive*

   A LinkedIn premium membership is not cheap. While there are different levels of membership, the one that most premium members opt for is the basic premium account, also known as Business Plus. On a monthly basis, the current cost is $49.95, although it is discounted to $39.95 if paid annually. A slightly more robust option is the Executive, priced at $99.95 a month or $74.95 if billed annually. Note that LinkedIn does offer a leaner "Job Seeker" account that is priced at $29.95/$24.95 monthly.

2. *Some swear by it, while others have found it to be a waste of money*

   Some premium subscribers are huge fans and would not go a day without it. Others report getting very little benefit. Before going into some of the benefits of the different memberships, it is important to know there is no true consensus on the premium options.

3. *The features are not much better than the free version*

   Each of the premium options allows you to see who has looked at your profile for the last ninety days. Without the premium option, that is limited to just the last five people, regardless of the time frame. Each also gives you several "Inmails" every month. Typically, with the free account, you can only send LinkedIn emails (called "Inmails") to those in your network. With the premium packages, you can send a limited number to people outside your network, such as recruiters and HR people. In addition, you will receive some other search functions that aren't available with the free account.

Those are the main differences between a premium account and the free account. The question is, is it worth $25, $30, or more per month?

Exercise:

LinkedIn is the most fertile ground for job seekers. It allows them to find open jobs, contact recruiters, make new connections at target companies, and showcase their abilities. Simply, if you aren't using LinkedIn to its full potential, you are probably missing out on some fantastic job opportunities.

The following is your LinkedIn plan to both achieve All Star status AND to attract more attention to your profile. This is a long-term effort, not a quick-fix. And you should plan to keep your profile updated and continue to post content long after you have secured your next position!

Part I: Be an All-Star

- Assure you have an appropriate picture on your profile. Make sure it is a tight headshot and very professional.

- Include both an industry you are in (or interested in) PLUS a location. Both of these are required for All Star status.

- List your education. Remember, you do not need to have graduated to include a school you have attended.

- Be sure you have a current position listed. For those out of work now there are still many options, including consultant to the industry.

- Update your past positions. Unlike your resume where you may only include the last ten or so years, include all of your past positions on LinkedIn. The more information you include on your profile, the more likely you are to show up in searches!

- Do you have at least three skills listed on your profile? Everyone can pick at least three! If you add new skills, be sure to ask people in your network for an endorsement to show those viewing your profile that you are a master of those skills.

- Work on getting to 500 connections if you aren't there already. Do regular searches for those currently doing the job that you are targeting and request connections.

- Have you connected to previous colleagues? And whenever you meet someone new, such as through networking and information interviews, add them to your LinkedIn network.

Part II: Get Active

- Set aside time each week to find and post content on LinkedIn. Pay attention to the type of content you post and the results you get. If one type of post garnered more views than another, use that type more frequently.

- With each post, try to find a reason to "tag" someone in your network so that your post is seen beyond just your own (This can be an excellent way to grow your network as well).

- Actively look at posts from other people and try to find a reason to offer a comment. Remember, comments are also viewed by the poster's network!

CHAPTER TEN

Resumes That Get Results

Don Bauder, CPRW

From the *History of the Resume*, by Cody Burdick, we learn that the word résumé is of French origin and means "summary." There is no specific date or person that can be credited with inventing the resume. Varying sources claim the resume was started by heads of guilds in the Middle Ages. Others say it was the famous artist Leonardo da Vinci. While the exact origin of the resume is unknown, it more than likely evolved over time.

Da Vinci is the first recorded person to use a resume. In 1482, Leonardo da Vinci wrote a letter to the Duke of Milan in an attempt to gain his patronage and support. Da Vinci's letter listed his skills and experience, the same thing we do today. Little did da Vinci know that he was starting a process that would continue to today and become an integral part of the hiring process.

Wikipedia tells us that, for the next roughly 450 years, the resume continued to be a mere description of a person, including their abilities and past employment. In the early 1900s, resumes listed things like weight, height, marital status, and religion. It wasn't until 1950 that the resume evolved into something more than words written on scraps of paper. By then, resumes were considered mandatory, and started to include things like personal interests and hobbies. In the

1970s, the beginning of the digital age, resumes took on a more professional look in terms of presentation and content.

There are several different types of resumes, but the most widely used is the Chronological resume where the candidate lists his or her job experience in reverse chronological order, covering the last ten or fifteen years. There is also the Functional Resume, where the work experience is sorted by skill function or job function.

There is a video resume, where a video of the candidate describing himself or herself is sent in a file to be viewed for a period of two to ten minutes. This form of resume is not encouraged by employers, because many load the resumes sent to them into software that organizes all candidates into the same format so that everything looks the same. This minimizes the effect of formatting, and lets each resume stand on content alone. Since video resumes don't fit the process and are time-consuming to review, they are generally discouraged by employers.

There is also the CV or Curriculum Vitae, widely used in Europe. In the U.S., the CV is generally used in academia and certain scientific fields. In this format, the candidate lists papers written, books published, research conducted, research findings, patents, etc., in addition to work experience. These resumes can run from several pages to fifteen-twenty pages or more.

The last general classification of the resume is the Federal Resume, for positions in the Federal Government. This resume focuses more on KSAs, or Knowledge, Skills and Abilities. Again, like a CV, these resumes can run much longer than the standard two pages. However, the hiring manager can rank candidates by these KSAs in the hopes of finding the most qualified candidate. The theory is, if you demonstrate having performed all the functions in a position, you are the most qualified. While this may appear to be logical, with the number of resumes being mailed to businesses today, it is not a particularly practical approach. Thus, the Federal Government now outsources high labor component functions such as call centers. They cannot screen and hire people fast enough using the long resume, and they cannot get enough candidates to fully list all KSAs to feel confident they have found the right candidate. Therefore, they use private firms to manage the risk of turnover and poor hiring decisions.

For the purpose of this book, we will talk about the Chronological and Functional resumes. However, I do need to make a distinction between a resume, and a resume that get results. We have already defined the resume, but the resume that gets results is written specifically to generate a phone call from the person to whom you send the resume. "But," you are thinking, "ALL resumes are sent with the objective of generating a response!" Yes, but the ones that get the response have something specific in them that appeals to the reader. This is why writing my own resume is so hard. I am focused on myself, but to get results, I need to be focused on the reader.

The resume that gets results is written specifically to generate a phone call from the person to which you sent the resume to.

During and after the recession of 2007-2009, employers had to layoff large numbers of people, and from 2007 to 2016, the economy did not grow above 2%. Low job growth and high unemployment meant employers received, in some cases, hundreds of resumes from job seekers in response to job postings. Employers had too many resumes to read to fill a position and fewer people in Human Resources, as many were laid off. They had to do something to improve the process of recruiting in an environment of resume overdose.

Many of the larger firms now scan resumes to be "read" by software rather than HR professionals to save labor expense and time. The computer program is written to look for "keywords," and only those resumes that have the correct keywords will be read by a human. For a large firm, this cuts out reading thousands of resumes per week. In an article by David Strom in *Looking in Tech*, it was found that recruiters spent exactly six seconds looking at a resume that has not been screened by a computer. This is the environment your resume is being sent to. So how can you possibly get better results when the resume is read by computer or gets a six second review by a human?

There are four factors you must consider before writing your resume:

- It's not about you – It's about them
- Tell a story to keep them reading
- Develop a brand to grab and create an emotional hold
- Quantify your skills to differentiate yourself from your competition

It's not about you – It's is about them

C. Bruce Flanagan makes this case in his book by the same title. What he points out is that the job search process is not about you, the unemployed or underemployed candidate; it is about them, the employer. Good sales people instinctively know this. When they enter a prospect's office, they look around the office for the clients' university, their hobbies, their family, and talk about that. People bond when talking about their interests, so the salesman talks about the clients' interests. You may hate football, but if the client loves football, you talk about that to bond with the client.

Human Resources people don't wake up in the morning wanting to find ways to help you; they wake up looking for ways to help themselves in their careers. They want to get through the stack of resumes without reading each one and find the perfect candidate very quickly. When you realize it is about them, you will search the job posting for their keywords, their requirements, and something about their company, and then strategically locate that information where they will see it in a quick visual scan.

Before you write your resume, read several job positions and job descriptions you are interested in and search for that data. When you learn that employers are looking for several key skills, put them in a prominent location on your resume. When they require certifications, don't wait until the bottom of the second page to show your certification with your education. Move it to the first page and bold it, so their eye scan picks that up. The quicker they see you have what they want, the greater the reason to continue reading. And you want them to read the entire document to learn what you can offer them.

If you are finalizing your resume and application and you read that the target company says, "We operate as a team to meet the needs of our customers," and you don't have "team player" on your resume, add it in a prominent place before submitting the resume. But only add it if you possess that skill.

When reading the job duties, you might discover that they want you to serve on cross functional teams to improve processes or solve problems. Make sure you include mention of a cross functional team you served on or, better yet, led. If they want something and you have it, it must be in your resume. You cannot wait until the interview to mention it. You may not get there. But never add something you don't have. That is falsifying the resume, and when you get caught in the interview, you will never get an offer from that firm.

It is not in your best interest to talk about yourself; it is your mission to MATCH yourself to the employer's interests and needs. That means you must tailor your resume for that specific job and company. I know, I hear the groan – I don't have time to rewrite each resume I submit. I will show you a format to use that allows you to change yourself for each employer, if needed, and how to do it quickly – in most cases less than ten or fifteen minutes.

Tell a story to get them to read the entire resume.

Throughout civilization, humans have recorded history by passing down stories from father to son, mother to daughter, teacher to pupil. In the early years, the stories were oral histories, and evolved into written histories. Why stories? Because a story is more interesting to read and understand than a college textbook in which you are expected to learn unrelated facts and events. The bestselling book of all time is the Bible. The Bible teaches its lessons in a collection of stories that serve two purposes. One is to pass down history, the other to teach right from wrong.

Politicians are famous storytellers because a good story illustrates their point very well and is easily remembered. When they want to make a point, and make it memorable, they will say, "That reminds me of a story about a farmer…," and the audience gets the point. Ronald Reagan, the Great Communicator, and Bill Clinton, known for his ability to bond with people, were speakers that won over audiences with their stories.

If you are thinking, "Why does anyone want to hear a story about me?," you missed the first point. Employers want to hear a story about the person they are looking for, because it is about them, not you. How do you make your story interesting to an employer?

The format (I will show you the resume format later) for story telling that I have used successfully for years is:

1. My name is …
2. I want to be a …
3. I'm skilled at…
4. My qualifications are …
5. I have accomplished…

The first point is your name and contact information, including cell phone, e-mail address, and LinkedIn address. If they like your story, make it easy for them to contact you.

The second point is what you want to do. It may be a title, several titles, a function, or description in their words. "Accountant" is great, but if you are sending this to a firm in manufacturing or construction, "Accountant with job cost skills" is better. Search for job postings and see what employers call the position, and what their number one need is. Combine the two, such as Project Manager/Healthcare, or Global Supply Chain Manager with Lean Six Sigma. Get their attention with what they want. A Supply Chain Manager is great, but if you are in international manufacturing, and you have Lean Six Sigma and global experience, the combined title really grabs their attention.

Many candidates list their skills in columns showing fifteen, twenty, or more skills. It is more effective to list the most important because, remember, they are just scanning your resume. You make it difficult for employers to see what they want quickly. Here is a good format to follow:

. . .

Project Manager / Healthcare

SKILL • SKILL • SKILL • SKILL • SKILL

. . .

If you list the skills that the employer wants with skills needed to be a Project Manager in Healthcare, you will catch their attention without boring them with a list of other, perhaps unrelated, skills. Communication, mentoring, and leadership are all directly related to the job title and are needed to be successful in the field. The person who reads your resume will realize this and keep reading. But if you list financial analysis, sales and operations, and other unrelated skills, the person scanning your resume will think the skills aren't exactly what they need and will determine that it is a good time to eliminate your "unqualified" resume!

Naturally, an employer wants to see if you have the qualifications to do the job and also wants to see this quickly without having to read about each and every job you have in your work history. Again, the hiring manager or HR screener is just scanning, but to get to this point they have found something in your skills they like. This section of your resume is vitally important, as the person looking at your resume is only prepared to read a few points. A good rule of thumb here is that three to five bullet points will give them what they want and need.

Don't lose their attention with non-critical items. Read the job posting and determine what the qualifications are. If there are three or four, it will be easy to incorporate these into this section. If the job posting includes a wish list of fifteen items, select the most critical ones. There may be two listed as important and two more listed as required. These four must be addressed. To build your resume that gets results, you should research qualifications for the position, paying close attention to what they want and require. Then list them in bullet points which talk about skills, education, training, how you operated, etc.

Here is a sample for a Supply Chain Manager who wants to serve on corporate boards:

SUMMARY OF QUALIFICATIONS

- 20 years of success with deep experience in supply chain, manufacturing, operations and the development and deployment of strategies aligned with corporate goals; includes conducting business in Asia, Europe, South and Central America, and the Middle East.
- Passionate about implementing Lean Six Sigma and other tools to drive efficiency into manufacturing, operations, and the entire supply chain.
- Analytical and skilled in leveraging data to manage remote locations, with an understanding of the key drivers of financial performance.
- Motivate others to lead change, develop positive internal relationships to create change and collaborate with suppliers, customers, and all stakeholders in understanding continuous improvement.
- B.S. in Industrial Engineering Technology, recent **MBA** in 2010, and trained in the use of VAVE (**Value Analysis/ Value Engineering**) by McKinsey & Company, a worldwide consulting company.

For a Healthcare Project Manager supporting call centers:

SUMMARY OF QUALIFICATIONS

- Quality conscious PMP-Certified Professional with ten years' experience successfully managing Federal, State and Local Government healthcare contracts; Accelerated Learning Master Practitioner / Adult Learning Certification.
- Alumnae of the prestigious (Name removed) *Series* which is a leadership development program designed for fast tracking and mainstreaming outstanding women into positions of influence in the public arena.
- Selected as Presenter at the 2007 *Governor's Conference on Service and Volunteerism* and Member of the Speakers Bureau for the *National Medicare RX Education Network*.
- Skilled at working with clients and teams to remove obstacles allowing teams to remain focused on the mission of utilizing business intelligence solutions to meet business needs; rated exceptional at last review.
- Technology skills include:
  - Adobe, Adobe Captivate, Plateau, Blackboard, SnagIt, HTML, Lectora, Visio, Dreamweaver and Stellent.
  - CMS: MARx, BERT, MBD, EBD, CWF and NGD

For a Sales Professional looking to grow Corporate Accounts.

SUMMARY OF QUALIFICATIONS

- Motivational leader that uses consensus to craft strategic plans, sets the tactical blueprint to reach sales goals, and has the listening skills to identify client need and sell the solution.
- Considered business savvy at identifying opportunities in the U.S. and international markets with a proven track record of launching new products, exceeding revenue, and increasing customer satisfaction.

- Has been promoted through the ranks of companies through sales and management positions while managing million-dollar domestic/international portfolios.

- Recipient of several awards including, **District Manager Award, National District Manager of the Year, International Distributor of the Year** and the coveted **Centurion Club at Fujifilm.**

You will notice in the examples above, using such techniques as italicizing, bolding, and indenting help identify critical, required, or important information relevant to the job. These are not just created for this book, either. The first example helped a client find a position in just four weeks -- after six months of no results. The second one used this information to orchestrate a move from Washington, D.C., to his hometown in the Midwest in less than two months. The third example helped the job seeker move quickly into a new position after he lost his job in a corporate takeover.

As noted earlier, the key to building a successful resume is to tell your story. The skills and Summary of Qualifications is where you should summarize your career into several bullet points that help to tell that very story. Telling your story is an attempt to match your skills, background, and education with what the hiring manager needs. This is, in reality, "branding!"

A corporate brand is the identity of a specific product, service, business, or what a person brings to the table. A strong corporate brand tells you all you need to know about a product. Think of Kleenex, McDonald's, Polaroid. Each of those need no further explanation. If I have a cold and need tissues, I can ask the clerk for Kleenex and she will know exactly what I mean. If you try to drive by McDonald's with kids in the car, those kids instantly know that they can get a "kid's meal" with a toy. That strong brand association causes an emotional reaction.

In the case of a supply chain professional (the first example above), the summary contains everything a company needs in a supply chain manager. The same is true for the Healthcare Project Manager and the Sales Professional. However, not all sales professionals are the same! This is why it is important to remember that your resume is about them, not you. Research your marketplace and determine what the market wants.

You will find, in some cases, companies would like to hire a "sales closer," while yet another might prefer someone who has a more consultative approach. These are different skills and you might offer both as a job candidate. Perhaps the position requires account management as well as relationship building. The establishment of your brand will allow the hiring manager to determine quickly if you are what they are looking for. Although it is tempting to any job seeker, you do not have to be all different types. A position posting spells out what they want and you need to focus in to show them that what they are looking for is you! They will see that you are exactly what they want in a quick scan of your qualification.

In my discussions with human resource professionals, almost every single one cites accomplishments as the top thing they look for most in a resume. In other words, they want to know you actually have the skill they need and can use it. Unfortunately, accomplishments are usually the most difficult item to get from clients when helping build their resumes. We are all taught not to brag and most of us simply don't keep accurate records of our past accomplishments, leaving it to the employer to bring them up at review time. Do not make this mistake! List your accomplishments regularly, even daily, and keep them in a file. You can use this file at review time to prove your value and show all your accomplishments for the year. Plus, if you find yourself needing a resume or a new job, the information is there for you to utilize.

You might think that is a great idea, but the fact is, you didn't do it at your last job and now you need a new job. What can you do now?

If you are like many people and didn't keep records of your accomplishments, here is a technique you can use to help remember what those were. I often ask job seekers to list the five or six things they are best at. Then, once the list is complete and they are happy with the items, I look them in the eye and say, "Prove it!" They will usually respond with such phrases as, "Well, I remember the time I ...", or "Well, I implemented this process ..." Think back in your career about awards. Were you named Employee of the Month? Did you make the President's Club? And don't forget comments that your supervisors made on your annual review. Did he or she say you were the best at something in the department? Were you a real pleasure to work with or to manage? If you can quantify an accomplishment and/or include comments from a third party about your successes, it implies proof of your skill to the person reading your resume.

Has anyone said something like this about you?

Quotes from client letters about Suzanne

- "She always goes above and beyond for me."
- "She was right on top of everything."
- "Thank you for going the extra mile on saving the money from this missed flight."
- "You are the absolute best."
- This client has called in before and states "how helpful you are and he likes to work with you."

Ideally, four or five accomplishments look best in your resume. Less than that and it appears you haven't accomplished much. More and it might make you look overqualified. You may not have enough to justify an entire section on accomplishments. But that's okay. The solution is to combine the qualifications and accomplishments together into one section.

Be careful not to have too many bullet points in any one section, as it begins to look like fine print, reminiscent of a contract, and much too easy to skip over. Try for no more than five bullets in any section. However, if you can't reduce the number to five, you can break up the section somewhat by using indentation to add white space to the page, making it easier to read and making sure that the reader doesn't skip over it thinking it is too much.

Here's an example:

SUMMARY OF QUALIFICATIONS

- Experienced travel industry sales, marketing and operations professional.
  - Team leader and motivator that builds teams to work together effectively.
  - Persuasive communicator that develops client and vendor rapport; achieve a 75-80% closure rate on RFPs.
  - Focus on marketing the advantages of a vacation or special offer that delight clients enough they feel special and return for future vacations.
- Multilingual in German and English; Bachelor of Arts in German with Minor in Spanish.
- Strong relationship builder, capable of partnering with clients, vendors, staff and administration; grew sales from $6 million to $13 million by negotiating favorable hotel rates and teaching the staff to focus on customer needs.
- Sharp financial analysis skills including accounting, budgeting and return on investment.
- Extensive travel in Europe, North and South America, and the Caribbean; worked overseas two years.
- Technical skills include 15 years' experience with Sabre and three years with Apollo, advanced skills in MS Word, Excel and PowerPoint and Intuit QuickBooks for small business.

As I said, four or five good accomplishments is perfect for this section. If they are recent or perhaps not terribly noteworthy, you can label the section "Selected Accomplishments." This is a great way to imply that there are more!

If you have some accomplishments that took a year or more to complete, you may consider labeling them as "Career Accomplishments." See the examples below.

Selected Accomplishments

- Used effective communications skills to avoid multiple fines at customs locations for infractions related to paperwork.
- At Transoceanic Shipping, was selected to review all contracts to clarify definitions, wording, and translation nuances better spelling out liabilities and reducing the company's risk.
- During the Hanjin Shipping crisis, had 150 containers of freight that were stuck in port with no ships; quickly obtained an aircraft and negotiated rates that preserved an acceptable margin on the acquired materials, and met the shipping deadline.
- Served on the Committee that achieved ISO Certification; reviewed all manuals to ensure completeness and compliance to regulations.
- Managed five international bank accounts with six figure balances to pay for shipments in local currency to avoid customs and exchange rate discrepancies that would delay shipments.

Career Accomplishments

- 2008 recipient of **President's Award** for Pharmaceutical/ Biotech IV Sales.
- Achieved hospital formulary coverage for injectable, buy and bill specialty product that became a **Top 50 Account Nationwide** while exceeding overall objectives by 110%.
- Developed territory sales plan to launch a new emerging technology medical device generating $1.1 million sales in first 6 months exceeding initial forecast by 25%.
- Penetrated the Mayo Clinic, developed a specific plan and won Clinic approval resulting in $1.6 million revenue.

This section of your resume by itself may take up one third to over half of the first page. But, to the reader of your resume, it is easy to review, and everything listed is something of interest. There are no large sections of small print, certain points are bolded and draw attention, and I even included a small font change in the skills section that "forces" the reader's eyes to those points. Everything is designed to make it easy to scan and quickly determine whether "I need to read this." In other words, it's time to settle down from scanning to reading.

COO / *Supply Chain Director* / *Director Operations*

STRATEGIC PLANNING • PERFORMANCE
IMPROVEMENT IN CHALLENGING ENVIRONMENTS
INNOVATOR • COMMUNICATOR •
FINANCIAL & OPERATIONAL ANALYSIS

SUMMARY OF QUALIFICATIONS

- Transformational leader that utilizes financial skills, business acumen and technology to resolve today's supply chain and operational bottlenecks to unlock business growth and profitability.
- Excels at putting together a distribution strategy, including layout of distribution centers, leveraging tools ISO / Lean / Six Sigma along with improvement project ROI, benchmarking and balanced scorecard metrics to provide a foundation for controlled growth.
- People skills include the ability to recruit, train, mentor and motivate the right people to execute strategic plans and obtain or exceed corporate objectives.
- Degrees include BA in Economics, BS in Mathematics with an **MBA** in Finance, Certified Management Accountant, **CPA** and a graduate of the Hoosier **Fellows Leadership Program**.

CAREER ACCOMPLISHMENTS

- Led 50% worldwide sales growth rate for 3,000 products, while improving gross margin 5% per year for Tripp Lite.
- Negotiated a seven-year $50 million convention contract for 60,000 attendees, earning the Indiana Business magazine's **BKD Indiana Excellence Award,** at FFA.
- Integrated ten worldwide acquisitions into a fulfillment network which included the design of a one million square foot distribution/ assembly center for Brightpoint.
- Automated a distribution center that was featured in *Materials Handling* magazine for Woods Wire.
- Earned inclusion in **Who's Who in the Midwest** and earned the **Indiana Governor's Award for Quality.**

But does a resume like this one really get results? After all, that's what you are after!

That very resume resulted in this note from one of my client:

Hi, Don,

I wanted to let you know that your resume format and content were very effective. I went from a 2-3% response rate to 6-9%.

I'm starting at the VP level with [Employer] next week.

Very best,

[Client Name]

This is the difference between a resume and a resume that gets results! The results gave this client THREE times more employer "reads" of his resume. He went from six months of looking to less than a month before finding his new position. Estimating his salary at $90,000, this resume put $37,500 more in his pocket.

Was it worth the extra time to get it right? I'll let you be the judge of that.

The next section in the resume is the Professional Experience section. This section should include your employer, the title of your position, the month and year you began with that employer, and the city of employment. Including the city aids employers in performing background checks. It is important to clearly name the employer you worked for, and if the company has been purchased or rebranded, include "now known as" or something similar to explain the name change. A resume that gets results often includes a sentence or two about the company. Such a description is easy to find by looking at the company's website. Company websites are crafted by marketing professionals and include useful descriptors such as "the leading company" or "a leader in." Including terms such as these is important because if you work for leading companies, you are a leader by association. If someone works for a top firm, we automatically think that person must be good! After all, top firms have a reputation for hiring the best.

A corollary to this is not to say bad things about a past employer as it reflects on you as much as the past employer.

If the company website isn't very useful, check Wikipedia for information such as revenue, number of employees, or anything else interesting to use. Many potential employers may not recognize your former employers, especially if they are smaller firms. So if you make them a leader or interesting, that makes you a leader and/or interesting too!

Production Manager
January, 2010-Present
ABC Company
Indianapolis, IN

ABC Company, with $50 million in sales, is a market leader in the manufacture and sale of widgets.

- This is where I begin the bullets that show what I accomplished for ABC Company.

Most typical resumes tend to say something like "responsible for a ten-person department," because that was the job description. If you list "responsible for" and talk about what you did, you are, in effect, saying that you can do that but not much more. That's no way to write a resume that gets results. And it is certainly no way to get a better job!

There is a formula you can use in constructing the professional experience section: SKILL – RESULT. For example, instead of saying, "I led a ten-person department," I might say, "I led a ten-person department and created a new culture of customer service that improved our customer satisfaction results from 25% good to 83% good." Who wouldn't want to hire that person?

Every employer wants to hire someone who is going to get results. Keep in mind, you must be truthful. Don't make up results just to fit the SKILLS – RESULTS formula. However, do always use a skill to describe how you handled your responsibilities. Don't just say you were responsible. Try to use more powerful words such as "led," "supervised," "administered," or "appointed to role model a positive attitude" – if that is true.

If you must use the word "responsible," use it once and no more.

A resume that gets results makes use of a variety of descriptive and exciting words. So make sure you have your thesaurus handy. Don't overuse terms like "developed" to talk about improvements you made. Find words such as "crafted," "created," expanded," "improved," or "re-engineered" to make your writing style more engaging. If your style is interesting, you are interesting. And if your style is boring – well, you get the point.

Soft skills are often overlooked, but not in a resume that gets results. Deloitte Consulting's 2016 survey of executives reported that 92% of employers said soft skills were equally important to technical skills.[23] And a LinkedIn analysis of soft skills most sought after and searched for included communications, organization, capacity for teamwork, punctuality, critical thinking, social savvy, creativity, and adaptability.[24]

As your resume begins to fill in and take shape, be certain that you remain conscious of the "white space." This refers to the places on the page where there is no typing. For example, consider looking at a contract with two solid pages of eight point type, as used here. The page is covered with printing, with no white space. Are you going to look forward to reading it? Are you likely going to read every line?

The fact is, we tend to scan and look for highlights in a document. The busier the document, the more we look for shortcuts. Remember when you were a kid and the teacher took you to the library to pick out a book to read? If you picked a book with solid writing, no paragraph breaks or blank pages, you thought, "This is too much work," and looked for a book with some pictures, page breaks, paragraphs, and maybe even a large font. A book that wasn't hard to read.

To be truthful, we still think that way. Don't scare the potential reader of your resume by making your resume look like a contract. Put spaces between sections, and try to never have more than five bullets in a row. If you need more than five (or maybe six), break up the grouping into two or three sections with headings and space before or after the heading. For example, under Professional Experience you might consider a heading of "Administration" and another of "Project Management." That will allow you to highlight your skills and add white space too!

Another very effective technique in resumes that get results is to add white space by right justifying. Your document is always left justified (each word begins directly below the word before at the beginning of each line). When you right justify, each line ends at

---

[23] Deloitte's 2016 Global Human Capital Trends report
[24] https://business.linkedin.com/talent-solutions/blog/trends-and-research/2016/most-indemand-soft-skills

the same place. To do this, your computer will automatically space the letters to spread out each line to start and end in the same place every time. This adds "white space" between the letters, which, while subliminal, is pleasing to the eye of the reader, and makes the documents "friendlier."

Compare the two paragraphs immediately before this one. The first is right justified. The second is not. Which looks friendlier to read and more professional?

Another often debated topic in resumes regards the font. Your resume should, ideally, feature twelve and eleven point fonts. In rare situations, a ten point font may be needed, but never smaller than that. In terms of which font, it is important to use one recognized by the Applicant Tracking Systems that will most assuredly be scanning your resume first. Times New Roman and Arial are always safe. These two fonts are often cited as "normal" fonts because we see them so often. You can choose other fonts that are close to Times New Roman and Arial, but avoid anything unusual. Even if the ATS can read it, you don't want the reader to look at your resume and say, "What is that!" Try to be neutral. Don't give the reader any reason to be uncomfortable with your resume before he or she even reads it.

Some job seekers in more creative careers (think of graphic designers, advertising people) more routinely use creative fonts. You should err on the conservative side. After all, the resume is a business document regardless of the position. And you should do whatever possible to avoid a negative reaction. If you are in one of those creative fields, sure, be a little "wilder." But keep it professional, too!

One past point: a page border is also a nice touch and looks very professional.

The last part of your resume that gets results is for Education, Training, and Associations. Begin with the lowest degree you have earned and move to the highest:

Associate of Art, Economics	1976
NEW COLLEGE OF FLORIDA	Sarasota, FL
Bachelor of Art, Economics	1978
NEW COLLEGE OF FLORIDA	Sarasota, FL
Bachelor of Science, Mathematics	1980
BALDWIN-WALLACE COLLEGE	Berea, OH
Magna Cum Laude	
MBA, Mathematics	2015
CASE WASTERN RESERVE UNIVERSITY	Cleveland, OH
GPA 4.0	

This section is pretty straightforward. List the degree, the graduation date, the college or university, and the location. If you don't have any education after high school, just list your diploma or course of study, graduation date, the school, and the city. Under each college you can list honors and your GPA. In the example above, the GPA is listed simply to illustrate where it would go. But if you have been out of college for five years or more you should have a substantial enough body of professional work that it is not necessary to list it anymore. For recent graduates, a GPA is typically expected.

After formal education, list Training. An example might look like this:

PROFESSIONAL SALES TRAINING

- Verizon Business – *Counselor Salesperson Approach* – Wilson Learning Systems
- TrustPoint – Trusted Advisor – *Problem Solving to Build Trust* – Tim Roberts
- S.P.I.N. for Major Accounts – *Account Management & Vertical Markets* – The Dartmouth Group

- Lushin & Associates – *Sales Training* – Sandler Sales Institute "Presidents Club"
- Consultative Selling in Utility Industry – *Building Long Term Relationships* – Ball State University

You can also list your Licenses and Certifications, or continued education:

CERTIFICATIONS & LICENSES
Business Communications Certificate, IUPUI, 2010 ◊
Human Resource Management Certificate, IUPUI 2010
Project Management Certificate, IUPUI, 2008 ◊
Indiana Real Estate Brokers License, 1985-2014

CONTINUING EDUCATION
CMA, Certified Management Accountant, 1986
◊ **CPA,** Certified Public Accountant, 1990
Hoosier Fellows Leadership Program, Indiana
University, Kelley School of Business, 2007

Whether you bullet point or center this section really depends on how much space you have to work with and your personal preference.

The last item on your resume that gets results is Professional Associations. This includes trade associations, awards, and any volunteer activity. You may decide to include speeches to groups or associations. Anything that shows you are active in your career field outside of your employment is fair game for this section. For example, if you are head of the finance committee at church and you are in a financial field, you should certainly include that. If you lead a Bible study and you are not in a religious-based career, you should probably leave that out.

A word of caution: don't include too many volunteer activities. The hiring manager may wonder when you have time for work!

It seems that everyone has an opinion on the "perfect" resume. In fact, I often joke that if you show five people a resume, you will get six opinions! No resume is perfect. No resume will get you a response – favorable or otherwise – 100% of the time. That's just not possible. But years of experience and analysis, successes and, yes, failures, have proven that the techniques in this chapter will be effective for you in your job search. A resume built on this outline is a resume that gets results. Isn't that what you want?

Exercise:

One of the keys to success in your job search is to be confident with your resume. While you will make small changes and adaptations for particular job applications, having a level of comfort that your resume is a good and true representation of yourself is crucial.

Write (or rewrite) a resume using the principles in this chapter. Does it show potential employers your "brand?" Is it clear what they get when they hire you? If not, keep working!

CHAPTER ELEVEN

Creating an Effective Cover Letter

There is an old joke about economists that if you laid them all end to end, they still wouldn't reach a conclusion. The same is true in your job search. As my good friend and resume writer, Don Bauder, said in the preceding chapter, asking five people for an opinion on your resume will yield six opinions!

Unfortunately, the same can be said about cover letters.

Cover letters used to be standard. Applying for a position without one was unthinkable! If you neglected sending a cover letter in with your resume, the hiring manager would – with every right – assume you had little interest in the position, had put forth a minimal effort, and, consequently, would likely approach a job with the same lack of enthusiasm and attention to detail.

Then came technology and millennials.

As you will see in the coming chapter on Applicant Tracking Systems, it is highly likely that your application will never even be seen by human eyes. It will be scanned by some faceless computer program looking for matching keywords and phrases that indicate, at least on some digital level, you are one of the few who would be a good fit for the position to which you have applied. Therefore, the logic goes, why waste time with a cover letter that either no one is going to see, or the hiring manager isn't going to care about because the computer already spit you out as a good candidate?

Which came first, the technology or the millennials, is a bit of a "chicken and egg" conundrum. Who knows if technology made millennials unable to focus and concentrate as long as their parents or if the millennials, who are primarily responsible for constructing the technology, were already wired that way and built computer programs to reflect their preferences. I can say that, in my experience over the last ten years or so, the human resource functions are primarily staffed by millennials and rely heavily on technology. So either way, cover letters are just not as crucial as they used to be.

As you have begun completing online applications, you have surely realized that many of the online submission systems allow you the "option" of adding a cover letter while still others have no provision for attaching one at all. It is rare today that a cover letter is required to complete an electronic application.

So what should a job seeker do?

In this chapter I will answer that question. I am also going to introduce a very special type of cover letter to you, one that will get read and, based on hundreds of trials with job seekers with whom I have worked, will increase your chances of getting an interview.

Should I Bother with a Cover Letter?

Frankly, there isn't any scientific evidence, like university double-blind studies and things like that, to prove or disprove that cover letters are read or not read. I would like to tell you with authority that 79.6% of cover letters are read, but no one really knows. That's because the process itself is subject to the individual preferences of the people in the HR department and the hiring manager. I have informally polled a few dozen human resource professionals and consultants on the question and have had many tell me that they still wouldn't consider an applicant who doesn't even take time to do a cover letter. Of course, I've had just as many tell me it is a waste of time – they get too many resumes to read the cover letters.

Still, there are some very compelling reasons to thoughtfully construct a cover letter and include it with each and every resume submission, whether online or in person.

The SHRM Study

SHRM stands for the Society for Human Resource Management, which is one of the premier member organizations in the United States for human resource professionals. To date, they boast over 285,000 members[25] and are an excellent resource for data and practices in the human resource space.

In late 2012, SHRM conducted a survey of their members on the issue of cover letters. While the responding sample size doesn't really measure up to statistical standards, the responses of the 582 members who completed the survey does offer some insight into the typical HR view of a cover letter.

Here's what the survey found:

Do people still use cover letters? Well, yes. 67% of candidates in the time period surveyed had included cover letters. That is, 67% or about 2/3[rds] of applications received had cover letters included.

Do HR professionals want cover letters? Kind of. 70% of the respondents stated they would consider a candidate for a vacant position even if no cover letter was presented. Another 28% said they would do so "at times." Only 2% said they would refuse to consider a candidate who did not include a cover letter.

The big news from the survey, though, is most likely the fact that 30% of the survey respondents said that they DO consider a cover letter when judging a candidate – assuming one is attached.

This information can be presented in a way that can be used to more satisfactorily answer the question of whether a job seeker should even bother with a cover letter. After all, there is a 70% chance that the HR staffer won't even consider what's in the letter, right?

> **30% of the survey respondents said that they DO consider a cover letter when judging a candidate.**

---

[25] "About SHRM," https://www.shrm.org/about-shrm/pages/default.aspx, Publication Date Unknown, Web, November 17, 2017.

The problem is, you have no way to know if the person looking at your resume is going to be in the 70% that doesn't care or in the 30% that does. So, by not including a cover letter on any resume submission, mathematically, you are at a 30% disadvantage to other candidates. Assuming your resume makes it past the computer scanning software algorithm and ends up in the hands of a live person, you have reduced your chances of going forward in the process by 30% compared to someone who took the time to write a cover letter.

Put simply, a cover letter does not decrease your chances of getting an interview, but it can increase them!

The SHRM study asked further questions as well. There is quite a bit of research available on the amount of time a resume is looked at by an HR professional but not much on the same topic for cover letters. The SHRM study asked those questions.

In response to the question of how much time HR spent looking at a cover letter, 83% indicated they spent one minute or less. Only 15% spent more than sixty seconds on the cover letter. (Apparently some didn't answer or answered, "I don't know.")

In fact, the survey maintained that the smaller a company, the more time they will spend on a cover letter. While the entire survey factored that 83% spent a minute or less, when only companies with 250 or more employees were considered, 52% said they will spend a maximum of thirty seconds looking at a cover letter.

The obvious problem is that no one, including you, can make someone read a cover letter if they simply don't read cover letters. However, if you include a cover letter and the person doesn't read it, it didn't hurt you. And if you happen to get one of those people looking at your resume that will read it if one is included, you are ahead of the others who didn't include a cover letter. It is another chance for you to make your pitch in another, persuasive way. On the "off" chance your application makes it to someone who is old school enough to require a cover letter, whew! Aren't you glad you did it?

So, assuming I have convinced you that cover letters are worth your time, not any old cover letter will do. By far, the most visually captivating, sensory-stimulating, informative, and persuasive cover letter is presented in a "T-format."

You may recall that, according to Glassdoor, the average job posting receives about 250 resumes and applications. To put some perspective on that:

Assuming each resume is two pages and a one-page cover letter is included:

That is a stack of solid paper 3" tall that the HR rep needs to go through carefully enough to find the four or five most qualified candidate.

That is equal to one and a half reams of paper!

Those resumes and cover letters, stacked one after the other would be 5,520 feet long. The Empire State Building in New York City is only 1,250 feet tall! That's almost four and a half Empire State Buildings laid end-to-end!

And, if the SHRM survey is correct that, cover letters get about sixty seconds max when they are read at all, that still means the HR professional would have to spend over four hours just reading cover letters. Even in larger companies in which the time reported was thirty seconds, that is still two hours of nothing but cover letters!

I hate to admit it, but there is no way anyone is doing that.

To further illustrate the daunting task facing the HR professionals tasked with finding the right candidates, try this exercise:

Below is an example of a typical, traditional cover letter. Set a timer for thirty seconds. Start the timer when you begin reading the cover letter, then turn the page at the end of the thirty seconds.

James Buckingham
11455 Elm Drive
Dallas, Texas 75001

February 24, 2017
MaryAnn Ramsey
Director, Human Resources and People Development

Noble Fulfillment Corporation
2000 Cannager Road
Dallas, Texas 75003

Re: Supply Chain Manager Position

Dear Ms. Ramsey:

This letter is to inform you of my interest in the position of Supply Chain Manager with Noble Fulfillment Corporation. I recently became aware of the opportunity through Indeed.com.

I have included a current resume which includes highlights of my skills and abilities in a number of supply chain-related areas. I currently work as a Senior Supply Chain Specialist with duties including inventory management, developing and maintaining cost lists, and managing vendor relationships. I also negotiate prices and terms with suppliers, vendors, and freight forwarders. I love interacting with clients and get along well with others in the organization.

I have worked in several different environments and I am quite comfortable with diverse people and situations. I have a strong work ethic and do what it takes to get the job done. I strongly believe that my experience, education, and dedication would be an asset to your company.

Please feel free to contact me at 469-555-5555 if you have any questions, or to schedule an interview.

Sincerely,
James Buckingham

Now, reset the timer for thirty seconds, turn to the next cover letter example, and repeat the exercise.

James Buckingham
11455 Elm Drive
Dallas, Texas 75001

February 24, 2017
MaryAnn Ramsey
Director, Human Resources and People Development
Noble Fulfillment Corporation
2000 Cannager Road
Dallas, Texas 75003

Re: Supply Chain Manager Position

Dear Ms. Ramsey:

I would like to express my sincere and enthusiastic interest in the position of Supply Chain Manager with Noble Fulfillment Corporation. Having been in the supply chain space for some time now, I am anxious to be a part of your well-respected company. Below I have listed my qualifications as they relate to your basic stated requirements.

Your Requirements	My Experience
1. Bachelor of Science Degree	✓ Bachelor of Science Degree from Northwestern University in Industrial Management with a 3.5 GPA.
2. Certified Supply Chain Professional	✓ CSCP designation in good standing since 2009. Currently serve on membership committee for Indiana.
3. Develop and maintain reliable suppliers.	✓ 5+ years of supplier management with no turnover of suppliers and <1% downtime.
4. Monitor and Assess Supplier Performance	✓ 8 years of successful supplier performance management with Xylow Logistics during period of 20% increase in production and 33% increase in revenue.

Based on my background, skills, and experience, I am confident my employment could benefit Noble Fulfillment Corporation and have a very positive impact on the employees and customers. I look forward to hearing from you to schedule an interview at your convenience.

Sincerely,

James Buckingham

What did you think about the first candidate?

What about the second?

If you were the HR staffer having to decide which one of these two candidates was going to be forwarded to the hiring manager for an interview, which would you choose?

Believe it or not, the candidates were not really different. Either of those cover letters could have been written by the same candidate. What is different is the *format*!

The T-Format

The second letter in the exercise is written in something called a "T-format." The T-format takes its name from the t-account that many of us learned in basic accounting courses. You probably noticed the large "T" in the middle of the letter.

The traditional approach to cover letters attempts to serve two purposes. First, to cordially introduce yourself to the hiring manager or HR representative. The second is to tell the reader a little more about yourself that, most likely, isn't evident on your resume. The problem with this approach is that times have changed. And the cover letter has too.

You have applied for a position, included a resume, probably completed an online application. The HR representative and hiring manager know you are interested. They don't care if you are cordial. They care if you are the right person for the job.

Even more important, however, is that the HR representative doesn't have time to read between the lines of your cover letter and get to know you. He or she has one goal at this point: determine whether you meet the job qualifications.

While meeting the qualifications will not necessarily guarantee you will be called for an interview, the opposite sure does! If you don't meet them (or, in the case of a traditional cover letter, the HR representative can't quickly determine whether you meet them), you WON'T get an interview.

The T-format is all about making your cover letter outstanding enough that it gets noticed, read, and, most importantly, makes the human resource staffer's decision about who goes forward easy.

The T-format cover letter offers several important benefits and has been proven in my clients' cases time and time again to be a crucial strategy in getting more interviews. Here are some of those benefits and reasons why:

1. *It does the job for the HR representative.*

   The HR representative's job would be much easier and quicker if there was a simple checklist that he or she could use to match your skills and experience with the job description. Most job seekers don't realize that this is, in a way, what is happening. The HR screener is given a checklist of elements that are required for the position as well as some that are preferred. As the screener looks at each candidate's submission, the screener scours the applicant's resume and, hopefully, cover letter looking for the information that can be used to check the appropriate boxes. If he or she doesn't find the information, the box doesn't get checked and the candidate never goes forward. Likewise, if the screener finds the information to complete the checklist, that candidate will at least be considered for an interview in which the candidate can make his or her case for the position.

The question is, given the 250 resumes and cover letters, the pile 3" thick on the desk (or virtual desk in most cases), how long is a screener going to look for those checklist items? The answer, of course, is not very long.

The T-format, in essence, completes the checklist for the screener, making his or her job much, much easier.

Notice on the T-format example earlier, the essential job requirements are spelled out and listed on the right side of the "T": five or more years of supply chain experience; two or more years of progressive responsibility in inventory management, etc. These are the exact requirements the screener is searching for to complete the checklist and this candidate has already done the work!

A little later we'll learn how to find those requirements for the letter.

2. *It is visually attractive and different.*

I have interviewed and spoken with many HR professionals, recruiters, career coaches, and others in my career. I am constantly surprised at how few candidates employ a T-format in their cover letters as well how few of the professionals, recruiters, and others even know what it is. That is a great sign for any job seeker who employs the T-format because that person can be pretty certain that their cover letter will stand out.

In a world in which people are more and more conditioned to digest little bits of information and have a more difficult time with detailed paragraphs and long articles (and the fact that many of the resume screeners are millennials who were raised on text messages and Instagram posts), people get bored very quickly. The T-format avoids that, as the entire letter is broken into easy to read and easy to understand morsels.

Go back and look at the page with the traditional cover letter, then look at the one with the T-format. Which would you rather read?

3. *It gives you another chance to make your case.*

Frankly, regardless of the format of your cover letter, chances are it doesn't include anything dramatically different than the information in your resume. It is likely stated differently and the format has changed, but the cover letter is still going to tout your accomplishments.

Resumes differ in just about as many ways as there are job seekers. Some use colors, some employ interesting fonts, some are chronological while others list things in order of importance. Some include lists of projects and programs; others, in the creative fields, may even include some artwork.

This fact is yet another issue for resume screeners. When each resume differs from another, no matter how good your resume is, the screener may simply miss something important. Maybe the screener expected to see it near the top while it was near the bottom of page one. In any case, if the screener can't find the information to match the job description checklist, your candidacy is over.

The T-format allows you to make sure that those important "checklist" items stand out. Even though the information is in your resume, listing it again in the cover letter, in theory, doubles the chance that the important items will be seen and you will pass the first cursory resume screening.

4. *It allows you to show off.*

As you have seen in the chapter regarding resumes, a good resume will include quantifiable successes. A cover letter using the T-format directly links these successes to the job requirements.

When you say that you have the five years of experience required, don't just list five years of experience. List five years of experience that resulted in completed projects, increased income, reduced costs, reductions in budgets, and so forth. It isn't just that you have done the job somewhere else. Tell the story about how good you were at it and let them realize that you can do the same thing for them!

Constructing T-format Cover Letters

The general format for the T-letter is simple and can easily be constructed by using the two-column option in any popular word processing program, such as Microsoft Word. The trick is to find the information in the job description to use on the right side of the "T" to make your information stand out and get you to the next step.

Here is a sample job posting for a supply chain role:

Manager, Procurement

Job ID #: 6777	**Location:** Indianapolis, IN
Functional Area: Purchasing	**Education Required:** Bachelor's Degree
Position Type: Full-Time Regular	**Relocation Provided:**
Experience Required: 7-10 years	

Position Description

- Directs and oversees many aspects of an organization's purchasing function. Collaborates with other upper management to develop policies and procedures related to the procurement of goods and services. Supervises many of the daily activities within the purchasing functions. Reviews purchasing decisions, orders, and vendor contracts. Oversees the ordering of materials and supplies from vendors. Develops, negotiates, implements, and manages commodity strategies that strengthen the company's supply chain Leads efforts to improve supply chain efficiency. Maintains product quality standards, and reduces costs. Evaluates and understands market conditions in order to develop global sourcing strategies to control costs. Assesses and recommends vendors. Manages ongoing relationships and resolves conflicts with suppliers. Strong project management skills with the ability to manage multiple projects with some supervision are desired. Familiar with a variety of Purchasing/Global Supply Chain concepts, practices, and procedures. Leads and directs the work of others. A wide degree of creativity and latitude is expected. Relies on experience and judgement to plan and accomplish goals Typically reports to top management.

Management Review and approvals: forecasting, negotiating, procurement planning, vendor management, writing contracts, pricing analyze. Contracts and negotiates pricing and terms with outside suppliers. Research potential vendors and compare their products, prices, and services.

- Develops and maintains reliable suppliers. Monitors prices by product and vendor to predict and account for financial fluctuations.
- Monitors and assesses supplier performance and advises management of questionable circumstances.
- Evaluates and understands market conditions in order to develop global sourcing strategies to control costs. Builds knowledge of the enterprise, processes, and customers.
- Collaborates with all purchasing and organizational functions on special projects and financial efforts.
- Ensures timely delivery of materials.
- Establishes goals based on experience and judgement.

- Adheres to unit and corporate purchasing policies and procedures.
- Manages ongoing relationships and resolves conflict with suppliers.
- Maintains a physical presence in the workplace.

Requirements

BS

This rather typical job description has lots of information in it. The purpose in writing the T-format cover letter is to identify the top few things to include. You cannot and should not include a line item in the T-format cover letter for every task and qualification in a job description. You want to pick the top three to five and try very hard to keep everything on one page.

Step 1: Eliminate the things that everyone has (or says they have).

Have you ever met someone who said they weren't a team player? How about someone who said they just can't get along with people? How would you feel if a candidate for a job told you that he hates goals and misses them virtually every time?

Most job descriptions contain requirements that are, in reality, meaningless. Everyone thinks they are a team player, everyone thinks they get along well with others. No one is going to say otherwise. And, these things are tough to prove with data one way or another. So they can be stricken as potential items in the T-format cover letter. In this example, "proficient interpersonal skills to work effectively with others," "collaboration," "creativity," and "ability to plan, etc." can be ignored. If those items come up in the interview, then you can talk about them.

Step 2: Identify the major responsibilities of the position.

In a typical job posting, the responsibilities of the position are often near the top and this example is no exception. Indeed, near the top there are nine bullet points specifically outlining the job responsibilities. Usually, the job responsibilities are listed more or less in order of importance to the job. So, in this case, "Develop and maintain reliable suppliers," is probably the most important function of the job. Likewise, "Monitoring and assessing supplier performance" is probably a very high priority. Read through the entire list of responsibilities in the job description to make sure nothing jumps out at you, but most likely, the top three or four are the most important and, consequently, the ones you want to consider including in your T-format cover letter.

Step 3: Identify the requirements.

Other than an entry level position, any job description is going to include certain requirements. Perhaps there is a minimum time required in a position or industry. There may be an educational minimum for candidates to meet. Most likely there are only one or two absolute requirements and you should not only include these in the T-format cover letter, but you should start with them.

In this example, the requirements include a BS degree and prefers an MBA or MS. This should be item number one on the T-format. It also lists certain professional designations that are preferred such as CPIM or CSCP. If this job seeker had one or both of these, that should be item number two on the cover letter.

So, by way of example, an applicant interested in this position may end up with a T-format cover letter that looks something like this:

Stephan Hobson
4550 Tall Pines Road Apt 6
Indianapolis, IN 46220

February 24, 2017

MaryAnn Ramsey
Director, Human Resources and People Development
Noble Fulfillment Corporation
2000 Cannager Road
Dallas, Texas 75003

Re: Supply Chain Manager Position

Dear Ms. Ramsey:

I would like to express my sincere and enthusiastic interest in the position of Supply Chain Manager with Noble Fulfillment Corporation. Having been in the supply chain space for some time now, I am anxious to be a part of your well-respected company. Below I have listed my qualifications as they relate to your basic stated requirements.

Your Requirements	My Experience
1. 5 or more years of supply chain experience.	✓ 7 years of successful supply chain experience with one of Texas' leading logistics firms.
2. 2 or more years of progressive responsibility in inventory management.	✓ 4 years of operations inventory management system resulting in documented cost savings of $250,000 through process improvement implementation.
3. Costing responsibilities.	✓ Extensive experience developing and maintaining cost lists. Instrumental role in team effort resulting in 15% productivity improvement.
4. Vendor relationship management.	✓ Managed all vendor relationships with suppliers to ensure current and future performance goals. Developed operating manual for vendor management.

Based on my background, skills, and experience, I am confident my employment could benefit Noble Fulfillment Corporation and have a very positive impact on the employees and customers. I look forward to hearing from you to schedule an interview at your convenience.

Sincerely,

Stephan Hobson

Advanced T-format Cover Letters

The concept of a T-format cover letter is not difficult and is a proven method to increase your chances of getting past a resume or application screening. However, there are a few more items that will help you make the most of this strategy.

Don't include too much.

Unfortunately, no one besides the screener knows exactly what is on that checklist that will move you to the next stage of the hiring process. The natural tendency is to include bullet points for almost everything in the job description. Resist that temptation. Keep it to one page and three to five points. If the screener sees the top few things in your cover letter (and it will stand out over others because of the letter format), he or she will at least take time to look over your application and not reject you out of hand.

Don't save it in a separate file.

When you are applying online for a position, which will be the case virtually every time, the biggest mistake you can make is to save your cover letter as a separate computer file from your resume. While many applicant tracking programs offer (or even request) submitting your cover letter separately, there are two very good reasons not to.

First, it is easier to ignore a cover letter if it is in a separate file. If the screener is one of those people who doesn't think cover letter are necessary, that person will not open and read it. They were already predisposed to ignore it and now you have added an extra step they have to go through to look at it.

Second, if you save the cover letter as part of your resume file, the computer system that will scan it for keywords along with your resume! This can dramatically increase your chances of getting past the applicant tracking system parameters and getting your application – and cover letter – into the hands of a live person.

Exercise:

Find a job description that interests you. It could be from a job board or a sample pulled from the Internet. Study the job description, identifying the key elements of the job – the major qualifications. Then write a T-format cover letter to match it. You don't have to actually apply for the position at this point, although you certainly can if you feel you are a good candidate.

Do this for at least three more jobs to get comfortable with the process.

CHAPTER TWELVE

The Applicant Tracking System

Remember the old saying, "It's not what you know, it's who you know?" Today, technology has flipped that adage on its head. As a job applicant, virtually every company now requires you to apply online and a computer program decides "what you know" before anyone even sees your resume or application.

This computer program has become the nemesis of job seekers everywhere over the past few years. This arch enemy is called the Applicant Tracking System, or ATS.

Of course, not everyone sees the ATS as a drawback. SHRM (the Society of Human Resource Managers) has published several articles touting the benefits, saying, "The ATS revolutionized recruiting by automating the storing and processing of resumes and by protecting companies against lawsuits through greater consistency in hiring practices." The explosion of ATS providers is further evidence that HR departments rely heavily on the technology.[26] Furthermore, HR professionals inside companies are not the only ones sold on the ATS. According to the website, Top Echelon, 75% of recruiters report using ATS software and of those, 94% believe it has improved the hiring process.

Maybe on their side of the desk!

---

[26] Zielinski, Dave, "Applicant Tracking Systems Evolve, https://www.shrm.org/ResourcesAndTools/hr-topics/technology/Pages/ATSEvolves.aspx, May 27, 2011, Web, November 17, 2017.

History

The ATS system is not necessarily new, having appeared in a few very large companies a little over twenty years ago. Most often, the first ATS is identified as a website developed in Canada called Viasite, which was a French-language job board for both candidates and employers with some programming built in that tried to match the skills to the job.[27] Today, there are more than 300 ATS systems used by 90% of companies in the United States. It has become very difficult to get a job without being able to play the game that the ATS has invented and refined over the years.

How it Works

An ATS system actually does more than just screen your resume for keywords. A good ATS system will automatically post jobs to various job boards, and even market the position through email and social media marketing. But it will also import resumes, parse the information into a common format making it easier for HR to compare candidates, and track the process for the HR professional in charge of filling the position. In fact, some ATS systems even assign numerical scores to each candidate relating how closely each matches the job description.

Drawbacks

That old saying of "garbage in, garbage out" is applicable to an ATS. The only way that the ATS knows what to look for in a resume and application is from the information it is given, typically the job description. Unfortunately, the job description is not always a true and accurate representation of the real job. Plus, many times the job description is written by someone in HR rather than the

---

[27] "A History of Applicant Tracking Systems," https://i0.wp.com/www.jobscan.co/blog/wp-content/uploads/2016/10/Infographic_History_of_ATS_06-31-1.png?ssl=1, Publication Date Unknown, Web, November 17, 2017.

hiring manager, and the HR person may not understand the job that well and be wholly unfamiliar with the terms and acronyms used. This means that the ATS may or may not be looking for the right keywords and experience. When that happens, good candidates – even the best candidates – may well get screened out of the process.

All ATS programs allow for fairly significant configuration by the company. This feature sometimes encourages companies to set all types of limits in the ATS in hopes of finding the "perfect" candidate. This "perfect" candidate almost never exists, and most often the candidate a hiring manager decides on does not fit the exact mold of what she thought she wanted at the beginning. So creating such a "tight" definition of a candidate can lead to lots of frustration on the part of the job seeker and the hiring manager.

Even CIO.com has lamented the fact that the ATS has impacted the hiring process negatively. And these are the people in charge of the systems! Capterra's J.P. Medved reports, the infatuation with ATS programs by HR is a "180 degree difference from what candidates see – they tell us the hiring process is frustrating, fraught with glitches, they have to manually enter information in duplicate, and then – poof! They're never sure if it even is reviewed by a human."[28]

Surely the technology is speeding things up, right? After all, the ATS is doing most of the work for the recruiters! Wrong. Glassdoor reported in 2015 that, in 2011, the average time from interview to hire was thirteen days. In 2015, it was twenty-three days: an increase of 77%! The same research showed that the larger the company, the longer the hiring process.[29] And, of course, that figure doesn't include the time from filing your application to the interview. That can be days, weeks, or even months!

[28] Florentine, Sharon, "Why your ATS may be killing your recruiting efforts (small case intended), https://www.cio.com/article/3028111/hiring/why-your-ats-may-be-killing-your-recruiting-efforts.html, February 1, 2016, Web, November 17, 2017.
[29] Chamberlain, Dr. Andrew, "Why is Hiring Taking Longer? New Insights From Glassdoor Data", https://www.glassdoor.com/research/studies/time-to-hire-study/, June 18, 2015, Web, November 17, 2018.

Strategies

While there is no "foolproof" way to get around the ATS gateway or to ensure you include every keyword that will allow your application to eventually be seen by someone, there are a few smart strategies you can employ to make the likelihood of moving past the ATS higher.

Strategy #1: Jobscan

As programmers improve and refine technology, invariably other programmers invent ways to help circumvent the new and improved technology. Think of hackers. Each time internet security is ramped up, hackers think of ways around it. Telemarketers routinely come up with ways to outsmart apps that help block their calls. The same is true in the ATS world.

One of the most popular and, in my opinion, most effective websites available to help you get past the ATS filter is called Jobscan.[30]

According to the website, "Jobscan is a tool that gives job seekers an instant analysis of how well their resume is tailored for a particular job, along with how it can be even better optimized for an applicant tracking system (also known as an ATS)." The Jobscan team studied the algorithms used by some of the most common ATS programs and built its own algorithm to predict how well each scanned resume will do within the ATS. Of course, it isn't perfect. After all, each ATS allows for significant customization which no one can predict.

The process with Jobscan is quite simple. You cut and paste the job description from the posting you are interested in, then cut and paste your resume right next to it. By clicking "Scan," the program does its work and you receive an immediate printout showing, both numerically and in a narrative, how closely you match the job. The site recommends aiming for an 80% or better match rate.

---

[30] You can access Jobscan at <u>jobscan.co</u>

CREATE NEW SCAN

Paste the text of your resume in the left box below. Then, paste the text of the job description in the right box. Don't have a resume and job description on hand?

TRY SAMPLE RESUME AND JOB

STEP 1: PASTE RESUME or UPLOAD RESUME

STEP 2: PASTE JOB DESCRIPTION

SCAN

Make my resume searchable to recruiters

MATCH RATE

62%

ADD MORE MISSING SKILLS INDICATED BY ✓ INTO YOUR RESUME TO INCREASE YOUR MATCH RATE TO 80% OR ABOVE

RESUME WORD COUNT ✗

There are 1062 words in your resume. If you are not applying to executive-level, government, or Australia-based jobs, consider reducing your resume length to under 750 words to increase focus and for ease of reading by recruiters.

ADVANCED DEGREE ✓

This job does not require or prefer an advanced degree.

MEASURABLE RESULTS ✓

There are five or more mentions of measurable results in your resume. Keep it up - employers like to see the impact and results that you had on the job.

WORDS TO AVOID ✗

We've found some negative phrases or cliches in your resume.

JOB TITLE MATCH ✗

The 'Senior Veterinary Receptionist' job title provided or found in the job description was not found in your resume. We recommend having the exact job title you're applying to in your resume to ensure you'll be found if a recruiter searches by job title. If you haven't held this position, you could include it as part of your objective.

COMPANY ✓

Adding this job's company name and web address can help us provide you ATS-specific tips. Company: Amazon | URL: www.amazon.com

ATS Matched.

172

Jobscan offers users five free scans, and each month you are registered, you receive an additional five scans. Plus, you will receive emails with opportunities to earn more free scans by doing things such as posting about Jobscan on social media. If those free scans are not enough, you can pay a fee and receive unlimited scans. Presently, depending on the option you choose (length of membership), the cost is from $22.00 to $49.00 per month. You can cancel at any time.

Strategy #2 Word Clouds

Another strategy sometimes used by job seekers is called a word cloud. A word cloud is a graphic that incorporates all the words in a document, then makes the most important words bigger and lesser important words smaller. It does this by looking for repetition. For example, if you built a word cloud for a job description and the description mentioned required knowledge of a software program, that software program name would end up large in the word cloud. The theory is that, if a term appears frequently in a job description, it must be important to the job and, it follows, important to include for the ATS screening.

Here is an example of a word cloud for an event coordinator position.

As you can see, the words project, construction, planning, and process are in the largest font. Development and meetings are not far behind. These words are likely to be very important to include as much as possible in your application and resume.

Strategy #3 Attaching the Cover Letter

Online application sites generally fall into two categories: they either don't allow for the uploading of a cover letter at all, or they ask for the cover letter to be uploaded separately from your resume. Strategy number three is this: don't do either one!

We already know that many recruiters don't read cover letters and those that do don't spend much time with them. Given that information, do you really think that if you upload a cover letter separately from your resume, the recruiter, assuming you even make to a live recruiter and are not knocked out by the ATS, will take the time to open a separate file and read it? I doubt it.

Rather than upload a cover letter separately in an online application, paste the cover letter to the end of your resume before you upload the file. This has two very strong benefits.

First, it forces the HR representative to at least look at your cover letter, provided you make it past the ATS. Second, the ATS doesn't know the difference between your resume and your cover letter! So that means the ATS will can both your resume AND your cover letter for keywords and phrases. Your chances of being "passed" by the ATS increase because you have more information to draw from!

Yet another reason to always do a cover letter!

Strategy #4 Finding the Keywords

You have probably realized by now that the key to getting past the ATS scan is to make sure you have the "right" keywords in your resume (and cover letter!). But that begs the question: how can I know which keywords to use?

The answer is to look far and wide at job postings for the position you are interested in. Don't just look in your geographical area or even at the top companies you would like to work for. Start by casting a very wide net and finding as many job descriptions that fit the job you want. Compare them. Very quickly you will find certain terms repeated over and over again. (You could do a word cloud of all the different job postings, too.) The likelihood is very, very high that the keywords the ATS will scan for – and the things the HR representative will key in on as well – are the ones appearing frequently in the different postings.

Make sure that your application, resume, and cover letter have plenty of references to those keywords!

Strategy #5 Forget the ATS!

The fifth strategy takes us right back to networking. Companies like referrals for job openings from current employees. Indeed, many companies even offer current employees a monetary incentive to refer new employees to the organization. And, in most companies, a referral from a current employee guarantees a look from the HR representative. In other words, you can avoid the ATS altogether.

Since the ATS also includes a system that manages the candidates in the running for a position, you will most likely have to apply online. You may even get a rejection from the ATS saying you don't fit the qualifications. But don't let that discourage you. If you can network into the company and get your information in front of the hiring manager, whatever the ATS did doesn't matter. One hiring manager we know in a professional engineering organization readily admits that HR inadvertently screens out good candidates and he also admits that he is very open to having known contacts send him a resume directly from an interested job seeker.

Eric is a recent job seeker who experienced the typical ups and downs of the job search process. He had his share of rejections, too. One day Eric received a rejection email from the HR Department at a company to which he had applied. He had applied for the position online, but had also leveraged his connections to try to get into the company. He was disappointed by the rejection until the next day he received a call from the hiring manager requesting an interview for that very position!

The applicant tracking system had found something it didn't like (or didn't find something it was looking for) and automatically sent him the rejection. Yet the hiring manager thought he was a good candidate!

You may already know someone in the organization you are targeting. Contact that person, tell them you are interested in the job, and ask if they have any advice for you. Typically, that person will offer to submit your name for you! Remember, they often get paid if you are hired! If they do offer, go for it! If they don't make the offer, politely ask them if they would mind making sure your resume gets to the hiring manager.

If you don't have someone you know in the company, chances are pretty good you can find someone. The easiest and fastest place to do that is on LinkedIn.

Using the search function we looked at in Chapter 9, search for people that work for the company, preferably in a similar position to the one you are interested in. You may well be surprised that you are already connected to one or two people there. If you are, send them a LinkedIn message letting them know you are interested in the position, asking for their advice, perhaps even offering to meet them (for an informational meeting). And, of course, ask them if they would deliver your resume to the hiring manager. Very rarely will someone say no to a person they know.

Of course, we all have some LinkedIn connections that we don't know well. If you are not comfortable asking your connections in the company to deliver your resume to the hiring manager, asking for an informational meeting is an appropriate step. Often, if you hit it off, they will end up offering to make the introduction to the hiring manager after all!

If you only have second-degree connections in the company, that is, you only see people who are connected to one of your connections, the process is just slightly different. Reach out to your direct connection, tell him or her you are trying to network into a company with the hopes of getting a job, and ask to be introduced to the connection that works there. This is done on LinkedIn all the time. It is highly likely your connection will step right up and make the introduction. Once the introduction is made, simply ask for the informational meeting and get to know the person.

A former TNG member was a director at a very large, multi-national pharmaceutical firm and had a position open. He worked with HR to get the job posted and weeks went by with no candidates forwarded to him. Frustrated, he checked with the HR representative tasked with finding the candidates and was told there were no qualified candidates who had applied. Several more weeks went by and still no resumes to look at. Finally, he went back to HR and asked to look at the rejected candidates. In reviewing the rejections, he identified NINE candidates that he wanted to interview. Ultimately, one of them got the job.

Had any of those nine candidates networked into him rather than rely solely on the online HR process, they would have been hired!

Recall that in the chapter on the likelihood of different job search techniques, or "interventions" working for a job seeker, the most effective technique was being proactive, networking, and following up.

Exercise:

Remember, the most effective path to a job statistically is not to apply online or only to do so in addition to making a connection that can get your resume in front of the hiring manager, preferably with some kind words.

If you have already applied to some positions with no results, work to find someone in your network that can help you follow up with a "real" person. If you are just beginning the process and have not yet applied, work diligently to find a contact in the company or a connected person that can make sure you get considered.

Finally, from the academic study referred to at the beginning of the book, we know that being "creatively" proactive is extremely effective. Each week contact a company from which you either were rejected or heard nothing and ask if they know of other positions, either inside that company or even with competitors, that you might pursue. It will be uncomfortable, but just might land you the best job of your life!

CHAPTER THIRTEEN

Publishing Your Network Newsletter

We now know from decades of experience and academic research that, for most people, networking is the key to getting a job. We also know that most people dread it and few are good at it. But even for those that do it, grudgingly or not, one of the biggest mistakes typical job seekers make is that they make connections, perhaps have an informational meeting over coffee, ask for some help, hopefully get a few referrals into companies, and then fail to follow up. To the person you worked so hard to meet with, it becomes "out of sight, out of mind." In fact, those people will assume that you found a job if they don't hear back from you regularly.

There are several approaches to keep your name in front of your network. I will outline the two best methods in this chapter. You can and should follow up with anyone you meet through networking and continue that contact with a viral network update.

Follow Up

The ideal model in networking and informational meetings involves your meeting with one person who refers you to two or three more. Those people then refer you to others and your efforts grow exponentially in an organic fashion. Of course, it doesn't work perfectly as some will introduce you to multiple contacts while others will beg off and be no further help. But, on average, if you are regularly holding informational meetings and making sure that you ASK each person if they know one or two more individuals with whom you should talk, you will have enough people on the list to keep your informational meeting activity going for as long as you need it. In my experience, the individuals who run out of people to talk to do not ask each and every person for referrals.

Remember, there is an art to asking for referrals. Some of your contacts will come up with names willingly and easily. Most will need prompting. Rather than simply asking if there is anyone you can talk to, mention your target companies. If they don't know anyone in that company or companies, mention the job title and ask if they know anyone who works in that discipline. For example, "I am really interested in a position at Conglomerate, Inc. Do you know anyone that I might be able to talk to there?" If your contact does, great! If not, then follow up with, "The position I am looking at is in the accounts payable area. Do you happen to have any connections that do that type of work I could talk to about the industry?" This second question broadens the person's thinking but still targets it enough that they are not simply searching their mental Rolodex of everyone they know.

Whenever you meet with someone, a follow up is mandatory. Send the person a card or email thanking them for their time and information and letting them know that you will be following up on their contacts. Whether you send a card or an email is really up to personal preference, although many people believe notes are better when you are looking for higher level jobs. Also, it seems that older contacts appreciate handwritten notes more than younger people. Either way, make sure you send it immediately after you meet.

Within a short time, be sure to contact the referrals your connection provided. In addition, once you have made arrangements with the referral to meet, drop your connection another card or email thanking her again and letting her know that you and her contact will be meeting the following week. Then, once the meeting takes place, also let the contact know that you met with them and how the meeting went.

Whenever you meet with someone, a follow up is mandatory.

If, by chance, you are unable to get in touch with the referral, after a week or so, let your connection know that you have tried and have been unsuccessful. Don't necessarily ask the connection to intervene, but let her know. Often, the connection will become involved and try to broker a meeting anyway.

Viral Network Update

Jessica Stephenson is a Vice President for a company called ExactHire. ExactHire manufactures and sells, of all things, the applicant tracking system that is the bane of job seekers everywhere. But Jessica is also a very well-connected person who loves helping job seekers. And Jessica is a huge proponent of the Viral Network Update.

As I mentioned, one of the biggest issues in networking is keeping your network informed. But it is even better if you can keep your network both informed AND engaged. Ideally, you can work with your network in such a way that your entire network is also looking for a job for you!

It can be done!

Jessica's Viral Network Update does just that. It is a newsletter delivered on a regular basis to those in your network updating them on your job search progress. A weekly schedule is the most common, but some prefer a bi-weekly schedule. It keeps your name in front of them every time they receive your newsletter. No more worrying about everyone thinking you already found a job because they haven't heard from you.

Here's how it works.

Format

The Viral Network Update should have a limited number of topics included in each issue. The three basic sections should be interviews, applications, and networking.

The interview section will include a recap of any interviews you had the previous week. In addition, you will mention any interviews that have been scheduled but not yet held. Finally, be sure to update your network in this section on the results of previous interviews.

A typical interview section of the Viral Network Update might look like this:

- I had an interview Tuesday afternoon at **LabTest**. I met with the **HR Director, Lindsey Burris**, and the hiring manager, **IT Manager Dennis Carney**. I felt that it went well. The next step is a personality assessment test that they are emailing to me in the next day or two.
- I received a request for a phone screen with the **HR Representative (Julie Shamis)** from **Touring Consulting Group**. That is scheduled for this Friday at 9:00am.
- Regarding the interview I mentioned in last week's update with **Eastern Graphics**, I received word that they would like me to come in and meet with **VP of IT Services, Meghan Mitchell.** We are working on getting that scheduled now.

You should notice that each update is short and to the point. More important, you should notice that whenever a name of a person or a company is mentioned, it is in bold typeface. Many of your network members will skim your newsletter. Remember, they have jobs and families and may not have the time to sit down and study it every week. By using bullet points to separate items and bolding the names of companies and people, your readers will be able to pick these important items out more easily. This is especially true if a networker knows a person you mention since familiar names "pop out" of the text.

In the section on applications, list each of the positions to which you applied during the last week. If you can, include the name of the company and the position you applied for. Also, if possible, do a little research and try to find who the position reports to and/or who the hiring manager is. Include this name too, bolded of course! An applications section may look like this:

- I saw a posting online for a **Senior Developer** position at **IBM** in Portland. I submitted my application on Tuesday. I am not sure who the hiring manager is for the position.
- A networker let me know that **Amazon** has an **AWS Engineer** position available. The hiring manager is named **John Black**. My application was submitted Thursday.
- I was contacted by an IT recruiter about a possible position with **ANSET LLC**. The position is for **Help Desk Manager**. I submitted my application to the recruiter. The recruiter did not offer the name of the hiring manager.

Again, be sure to use bold typeface for each company and individual name included in this section.

The final section includes your networking activity. If you regularly attend networking meetings, include those each week. Whenever you have an informational meeting, that should be listed in this section. List the name of the person you met with (and bold it). (There will be some people who prefer not to be named so be sure to respect their wishes).

The networking section will likely look something like this:

- I had a great informational meeting with **Stephanie Crooks**, a director with **Community Hospital**. She has introduced me to **James Buttermilk** and **Hayley Dunaway**. I'm in the process of making contact with them now.
- I attended TNG last week. The speaker was a recruiter concentrating on pharmaceutical companies.
- I also held an informational meeting with **Gina Ball**, an **HR Professional** who owns her own consulting business.

In reality, the networking section may not be the most productive of the three in terms of getting help from your network. But it serves a couple important purposes. One, it keeps you accountable to your job search. It is embarrassing to send a message to your friends, former coworkers, and contacts admitting that you didn't do anything in your job search in the last week. Knowing this, you will naturally start thinking about your newsletter several days before you send it and make sure you have some good activity to share. Second, people want to help people that help themselves. If a networker sees very little activity on your part, they won't go out of their way to help you on their end. But if they see you busting your butt week after week, they will be much more likely to offer help in your job search.

Intro

Of course, just sending a weekly email with some bullet points isn't enough. Each of your issues should include a header thanking your networkers for their willingness to be part of your Viral Network Update, for their help in your job search, and letting them know the type of company and/or position you are looking for. There is nothing wrong with using the same heading each time. You don't have to spend time revising it week after week. Your header may read something like this:

"Thank you, Viral Networker, for agreeing to help me in my job search. Most jobs are secured through networking and your willingness to help is the key to my success in finding my next great position! If you see any company or name listed in this email that you know or have connections with, I would appreciate an introduction. If you can put in a good word for me, that's even better!"

Attachments

To each issue of your Viral Network Update newsletter, be sure to attach your basic resume and, if you have one, your marketing piece.

Encourage your networkers to share either or both with anyone that they think might be able to help you in your search.

Building Your Email List

We all get way too much spam and the last thing we want is to generate more. Don't simply send the Viral Network Update to everyone you know or even all of your LinkedIn contacts. You must give people the option of receiving it. Luckily, there is a process you can follow to ensure that your network is interested in receiving it and you are not running afoul of any anti-spam laws and regulations. In addition, some Internet Service Providers have programs that block emails that "look like" spam (i.e., ones that are sent to more than a set number of people at a time). Ensuring that your network is interested in getting your update is key to getting around each of those obstacles.

Begin by identifying fifty people that you know, have relationships with, and you believe may be able to help you in your job search. These may be family friends, former co-workers, old bosses, neighbors, even customers and suppliers. Put a message together explaining what you are planning to do and simply ask them to "opt in." Your message might be similar to this one:

Shawn –

You may know that Axxent, the company I worked for the last three years, recently reorganized and my position was eliminated. As part of my efforts in securing a new position, I am planning to send a weekly newsletter to a select group of my contacts letting them know of my activity. Since networking is the most effective method of finding a job, my hope is that you, or one of my other networkers, might see something in my activity and be able to help.

May I include you in my newsletter? It will come once a week and you can opt out anytime you wish.

I respect you and hope you will agree to be part of this project! Please let me know.

Sincerely,

Jill Graham

Don't expect all fifty to jump on board. Perhaps forty will, or maybe only twenty-five. That's okay. This is only the beginning for building your Viral Network.

Use your email service to create a list that you can email to each week. By sending the message to yourself (in the "to" field) and including the list as a blind copy (the bcc field), you are not giving out everyone's email address to all of your contacts. You don't want to invite more spam for the people that are trying to help you!

Also, as you hold informational meetings, in addition to asking who else you might meet with, get into the habit of asking if the person would mind being part of your Viral Network Update. Although you can't force anyone to read it, virtually everyone will agree if asked. One of our TNG members started with forty on his and, over time, had over one hundred people on his weekly distribution list!

Effects

The ultimate goal of your entire job search journey is, of course, to get a job. The Viral Network Update is certainly no exception. However, you will find that it also does a couple other good things for your job search.

First, as I said, it keeps your name in front of people and keeps your search relevant to them. With busy lives, your job search may not be foremost every day to your networkers. But it will be at least once a week!

Second, the format lends itself to both those who will diligently read the message each week and to those who will only skim it. Either way, names will jump out and connections will be made. I guarantee you will have networkers respond that they know the person you are interviewing with, or someone in the company you applied to. We are all connected to others and the Viral Network Update serves as a multiplier to your network.

Third, job searching is tough. It is related to increased depression, anxiety, and even divorce. Anyone who has been through it knows it is a roller coaster ride. When you get a call for an interview, you feel great! When you don't hear back from a company, or worse, get a rejection, your mood tanks. One of the beautiful effects of the Viral Network Update is that you will receive positive encouraging feedback from your network on a regular basis. Hardly a week will go by without you receiving a note or two from a networker telling you that you are doing the right thing, or to keep your head up, or that they are proud of all the hard work you are doing. Even though these are not necessarily furthering your path to your next job, they can be spiritually and emotionally invaluable.

Finally, you will receive leads on jobs that you didn't know about from your network. Remember, many jobs are not published at all, or only as a last resort when a company can't find an internal candidate or a referral. Many people in your network know of positions at their company and others that haven't been publicized. By keeping everyone apprised of your job search activities, you are keeping yourself in the mix for those positions when they arise. It will become somewhat common for you to receive job leads from your network.

Why Doesn't Everyone Do This?

Of all the job search techniques, the Viral Network Update is one of the most effective. It is also one of the least used. Remember Jessica Stephenson, the one who is an ardent promoter of this strategy? Even she admits that of all the people she recommends it to, perhaps one in five actually does it. That's just 20%.

Of course, that's good news for those that do it since there is little competition for the time and attention of your networkers! Chances are they will only get one newsletter like yours each week.

The reason for such a low adoption rate is simply the stigma of being unemployed. Many people are just uncomfortable telling the world that they don't have a job and even more uncomfortable telling everyone that they can't get another job easily. We would all like to be so good that the world is beating down our door with opportunities. Unfortunately, no one is that good.

The fact is there is really no way for you to work your network to its maximum potential without letting people know you are looking! They won't think anything less of you and, highly likely, will want to help you. But they have to know you need the help. Plus, people take great pride in helping others find a new job. They feel useful and good about themselves because they took part in placing you in your great new job.

Indeed, during your job search you will actually find that many people have been through the same process, often involuntarily. These people will become your empathizers and champions, willing to help however they can!

Exercise:

Consider starting a Viral Network newsletter. You may not be comfortable letting everyone know about your situation so this technique is not embraced by everyone. However, it is a powerful tool. If you are uncomfortable with a wide distribution, perhaps only include close family and friends at first. If you think it is working, you can always invite others into the network!

CHAPTER FOURTEEN
Following Up

N ow what? You found what looks like a great job, hopefully networked your way into the company using your connections, even made sure that the hiring manager sees your resume instead of going through the uncertain online submission and hoping and waiting! You are done, right?

Not quite.

Many people call applying for jobs a black hole, for good reason. Even when you do everything you can to make sure that your resume and application get seen by the right people, today the most common response is, quite simply, no response. At least, not right away. To be fair, certainly many people are busy with their own jobs and the demands on the hiring manager may be exacerbated because she has an open position she is covering. Who has time to do their job, plus study a few hundred resumes, schedule interviews, make a decision, prepare an offer, etc.? Often you will find that the decision only really begins to move forward when the opening becomes critical, at least to the hiring manager.

This could actually be good news for you, however. Most people fail to do one of the most important tasks in successful job seeking: following up.

I want to remind you of the academic research we looked at earlier. The most effective job search technique (intervention) was

Dale Hinshaw, Tom Faulconer, and Mike Johnson

proactivity on the part of the job seeker. Yet almost no job seeker performs this important phase of the search.

What are some ways that you can proactively follow up to enhance your chance of getting the job you want? Here are a few to consider.

1. Thank yous after EVERY contact.

   It is hard to believe, but the number of job seekers who send thank you notes to those that they interview with is actually fairly small. Most people go through an interview, then sit back and wait for the next step. That's a mistake you shouldn't make.

   If you have a phone screen OR an in-person interview, follow up immediately with a thank you note to all the people involved in the interview. This requires making sure you have business cards with contact information or an email address for every person.

   There is a substantial school of thought that says you should send thank you notes through the U.S. Mail rather than an email, as a hiring manager is likely to get very little personal mail. This personal touch, the theory goes, will make your candidacy stand out and make you memorable as the process continues. While I certainly agree with that philosophy, I will also admit that there are more and more situations in which an email is sufficient or even preferred. If you are interested in a high-tech or IT job, sending a thank you note through the mail may well make you appear old fashioned. Likewise, if the interviewer(s) is in his thirties or younger, you may appear out of date and out of touch, as they have never really had any use for "snail mail" in their young lives!

   If you do follow up with a note through the mail, here are some good tips to consider:

- Hand write the note. A typed or printed thank you is just not as effective in creating the image that you are personable and interested and willing to go the extra mile to get the job.
- Send the note as soon as possible. A good trick is to go to any interview with thank you notes in hand. As soon as the interview is over, go to a library, a coffee shop, or even sit in your car and compose the notes while the information is fresh.
- Customize each one. Assume the interviewers will compare notes because they will. If you write the same note to every person it will not be looked on favorably. As you write each note, strive to mention something personal from the interview. Reference a question or comment that the person brought up. Compliment them if you can appropriately.
- Plan ahead. Don't just bring thank you notes with you; bring <u>pre-addressed, stamped</u> envelopes for each of the people you will be interviewing with (plus an extra or two in case there are some last-minute additions as often happens, especially when an interview goes well). As soon as the notes are finished, put them in the envelopes and mail them. If you can find a mailbox near the office where you interviewed, use that, as your notes will most likely arrive the next day. I have heard stories of job seekers that have a late afternoon interview, do thank you notes and drop them in the mail immediately, and the notes are waiting on the desk of the interviewers the next morning. That's impressive!

Even if you interview with the same person multiple times, send a thank you after each meeting (but not the same note every time).

Lori is a talented medical device professional with an MBA and a strong track record at a large pharma company. A couple years ago, Lori found herself in the job market and became a regular attendee at TNG. Lori faithfully followed the process outlined and sent handwritten thank you notes to every interviewer.

After a few different interviews at different companies, Lori had an interview with an organization that she really liked and wanted to work for. During the interview process, the discussion moved to the company's global positioning. Rather than just send a generic "thank you" note from a stationary store, Lori worked to find something more fitting. She quickly found notes that featured a map of the world on the front. She then wrote each person a customized note referencing the company's position in the world and how she could positively impact that position.

Lori got that job and credits her careful selection of appropriate note cards for sealing the deal!

2. Follow up with all your pertinent contacts.

Chances are, if you get an interview, it is because you networked with previous connections and/or made some new ones. Another crucial activity that is very often overlooked is keeping those people informed along the way. Remember, if a person had enough influence to get you to the hiring manager, they still have enough influence to "sell" you during the process.

You should send an update to your pertinent contacts every two weeks, letting them know that you are still in the process or if any activity has taken place. Also, any time there is a major event, like an interview, you should send them a message.

While handwritten notes are typically appreciated by anyone, don't feel like you have to do handwritten, mailed notes to your contacts. Emails will usually suffice.

3. Don't be afraid to drive the process.

One of the most difficult issues job seekers face is overcoming that feeling as if they HAVE to have this job, that they need the job more than the company needs to hire them. That's simply not true. It is an understandable feeling, but not true. The company has already sent the word out, even potentially spending a fairly substantial sum of money for recruiters and advertising, to let the world know that they need someone like you. In the end, hiring is a transaction, not a charity. You offer the company something it needs and it gives you something you need (a challenge, a purpose, and a paycheck!).

There is no reason that you should have to sit idly by the phone or computer day after day waiting for a message. There is no reason whatsoever that you cannot initiate contact on a regular basis and inquire about the process. You may remember earlier in the book when I said that follow up will not make the company like a bad candidate or hate a good one.

Make it a priority to contact the hiring manager or HR representative every so often. Two weeks is usually a good interval, as more frequent contact can be annoying to a busy worker. An email or phone call (even leaving a voicemail) is perfectly acceptable in which you simply state that you are excited for the opportunity, that you were wondering where things were in the process, and perhaps mentioning that you are still pursuing some other opportunities but would really like to work for that company. You also might keep a little variety going – perhaps alternate an email and phone call/ voicemail message.

Of course, job seeking is really marketing; you are marketing yourself instead of a product. But there is a very well-known and effective maxim in marketing relating to scarcity. People put a premium value on things that are in short supply. Have you ever noticed that, around Thanksgiving each year, a story appears saying that there is likely to be a shortage of a hot item this coming Christmas? Do you really think that's true? Well, whether it's true or not is a moot point. People clamor for that item like water in the desert!

By letting the company you are interested in know – subtly – that you are talking to other companies, you are creating that same type of scarcity – and, in effect, potentially driving up your value in the mind of the hiring manager.

Sure, it's hard to follow up sometimes. You don't want to turn them off to you because you keep calling and emailing. But, frankly, my friend, either they want you or they don't and all you are doing is putting a little pressure on them to close the deal.

Tony was a TNG member who worked very hard to find a position. After a few months of frustration, he found himself interviewing with two different companies. One had been stringing him along for several weeks involving interview after interview. The other, which is the one that Tony really wanted to land, had just popped up. In fact, at that moment, Tony had only submitted a resume and application and had a phone screen. He didn't even know if he would be selected for an interview!

The company that Tony had been interviewing with contacted him and made him an offer. The offer was respectable and Tony would probably have taken it. But before making his decision he contacted the other company, the one with which he had only had the phone screen, and told them that he had an offer from someone else but that he really wanted to work for them instead. They rushed him through the interview process, made a decision, and he was hired by his first choice.

Chances are, if Tony hadn't pushed the issue, it might have been weeks or even months before he heard from that company. Instead, he landed the job, more or less circumventing the process and heading off other potential candidates. If Tony had let the company take its time, they may well have brought in more candidates, even looked for someone that would do the job cheaper. But the potential competition drove the decision.

Exercise: For each and every interview, including informational interviews, send a thank you note and reflect that activity on your tracking sheet.

CHAPTER FIFTEEN
Preparing for the Interview

It is often said that finding a full-time job is itself a full-time job. And learning and applying the tools and techniques presented in this book can be time consuming. Customizing each resume, preparing a cover letter in the T-format, making connections to help you inside the company; these take time and hard work.

Unfortunately, all that work is not going to get you a job. Those things will help you get an interview. Once you are selected for an interview, there is more hard work on the horizon. But, thankfully, this is the work that will actually secure you that job!

The fact that you were selected for an interview not only puts you in select company (remember, most people don't even get this far statistically), it also means that the business you are interested in is interested in you. HR professionals and hiring managers don't have time anymore to interview people for the sake of being nice. They interview the people that they feel have a legitimate shot at getting the position and making a positive impact on the organization. You are in that group!

You can think of the interview process as having three distinct phases: the preparation, the presentation, and the follow-up.

Preparation

When you get the phone call or the email requesting an interview, you can be assured that someone (or maybe more than one person) has seen your resume. They are acquainted with you and your accomplishments. They may have even looked at your LinkedIn profile to see additional information about you. (Remember, your LinkedIn and other social media should tell a consistent story with your resume and applications. If you are applying for a position as a sales manager but your LinkedIn profile talks all about your human resources past, that's going to be a red flag for the company). The interview is not being scheduled to rehash your resume. You are being called in to answer three major questions for the employer.

Can you do the job?

There are only two times in a person's life when they are perfect. One is their obituary – no one says anything bad about you when you pass away! The second is your resume. You resume only includes the best and stellar information about you. You are trying to get a job, after all! Companies know that about resumes, so part of the interview process will be digging deeper to see if you really know the stuff you say you know on your resume. In other words, do you have the requisite skills to perform the job?

As part of the deeper "dig" into you and your experiences, the company will also try to determine the level, or depth, of your knowledge in certain areas. A job applicant's resume may say that she is proficient in project management. But this company uses Agile project management. They will want to see if your project management experience includes that methodology. So, do you have the knowledge needed to perform the job?

The interview is not being scheduled to rehash your resume!

To pass the "interview" test, you will also need to be able to show that your experience on your resume has produced results in the past. A software designer who has worked on ten projects but never brought one to completion is not as attractive as one who has brought three to the finish line on time and on budget. Yet both will claim extensive experience and knowledge in the area on their resumes. Can you produce results?

That old, tired saying that nothing is constant except change is, sadly, quite accurate. Companies that don't keep up with the changes in technology, the preferences of the workforce, and innovation in products die more quickly than ever before. The company you are interviewing with knows this and they are interested in employees who are adaptive to changing conditions and requirements. The job you are hired for today will likely be much different than the job you are doing in five years. How adaptive are you to change?

Will you do the job?

This may seem like a silly question to many people. Of course you will do the job! Why would you be working so hard to get it if you weren't interested in actually doing it? But, the truth is, there will be some decisions you will make along this path to employment that may move you to decide you don't want the job after all. For example, you may find out that the job pays less than you expected. Or that the job requires work on nights and/or weekends. These could be "deal breakers" for you. The company wants to determine that now rather than later.

In the interview process, you will be asked questions designed to gauge your level of interest in the job. Many people apply for jobs because they need a job. Or for the interview experience. Or because they think it pays well. Your interview will involve determining whether you have a genuine interest – even better, a passion – for the job. Interest and passion can often make up for deficiencies in other areas such as experience and education. Are you really interested in this job?

Everyone is nervous in an interview. That's human nature. So if you are a bit nervous, don't worry. Every other candidate the company is talking to is nervous! But be sure not to clam up during the interview. Companies want dynamic, creative people, filled with passion! And the interview is the only time you can show it off. Are you showing your energy during the interview?

As I mentioned, salary can become a sticking point for some candidates. The job you are interviewing for may be your dream job, but if the pay isn't enough to cover your bills, you are probably going to have to decline. Every job seeker has a mental picture of what a job pays when he applies. Likewise, every company has a number, or a range, they expect to pay to fill the position. During the interview, the company will often try to see how close together those two positions are.

Companies want dynamic, creative people, that have passion! And the interview is the only time you will have to show it off. Are you showing your energy during the interview?

The salary discussion can be a very tough time during the process. Job seekers are counseled not to bring it up early and when the company is the one to bring it up, job seekers are often scared to blurt out a number, concerned it is too high or too low. We'll deal with that later in the book, but don't be surprised when the subject comes up. Are your salary expectations consistent with the employer's?

Just like businesses can't stay static and survive, companies want employees with ambition and the desire to grow and change in the future. Your resume may be a great representation of what you have done in the past, but the interviewer wants to see where you want to go in the future. The tried and true standard interview question, "Where do you want to be in five years?," is still around and pertinent.

This question can require a delicate answer. Giving an answer that can be interpreted as your wanting to move on to another company will not be received well (even though, statistically, it's likely true!), and giving an answer that makes it sounds as though you are gunning for the boss's job won't be ideal either. So the best answer is to concentrate on your personal development rather than naming a position you would like to have. Perhaps you are interested in using the company's tuition reimbursement program to further your professional education. Or a professional designation that is related to the job might be a good answer. What are your plans for future career growth?

How well do you match the environment?

The fact that everyone is unique may be an oxymoron, but it is true! We all have different styles, likes and dislikes. Those traits and preferences carry over into the job. Companies want employees that have work styles consistent with others in the organization. A person who likes (or needs) the structure of a nine to five punch the time clock-type job is not going to be successful in a millennial-dominated startup where most of the people work from home and others come and go at all hours of the night. In many start-ups, the concept of an open office environment has become popular. Can you work effectively in that environment? In other words, what is your work style? Is it compatible with the company and the group you will be working with?

So much of a company's culture is dictated by what the company does. Every company has certain values, whether or not the company explicitly states them. Believing in the mission of a not-for-profit is important to the organization when hiring new employees. Even in a for-profit business, believing in what the company does is a big plus. Are you aligned with the company's culture and values?

A current business buzzword is "matrixed." Companies are often described in job descriptions as matrixed or highly matrixed environments. Realistically, many say that but may or may not be that way. A matrixed business is one in which communication flows up, down, and across levels, rather than following the old-style chain of command. To survive and thrive in this type of environment, an employee must be able to communicate on many different levels and through many different media. That company will likely want an employee who is comfortable talking shop to the vice presidents and can explain concepts to others verbally, in writing, and in presentations. These communication skills are important in any job and will serve you well. The interviewer knows that and is looking to see if you can deliver. How well do you communicate with others?

Finally, just as I compared hiring to dating early in the book, just like in matchmaking, companies are looking for chemistry. You are going to spend more time at work than awake and at home with your family. Finding that connection between you and the company and between you and your potential boss and coworkers is imperative. There is a saying that people do business with people they like and trust. Companies also hire people they like and trust. What kind of chemistry is there between you and the employer?

Be aware though that, like dating, such chemistry may not be evident immediately. It may become more apparent and more intense as the process continues.

The Stages of Interviewing

Interviewing isn't as simple as sitting down with your potential boss for an hour any more. Given the risks associated with making the "wrong" hiring decision, most companies now involve a much more complex process of interviewing to ensure they hire the best candidate for the job. This newer version of the interview process may include several steps.

Screening Interviews

If the HR department looks at your resume and thinks there is a good chance you can do the posted job, you may receive a request for a screening interview. Often this request will be in the form of an email. Sometimes, a phone call will be the preferred method.

The most considerate HR professionals will request that you

schedule a time convenient for both of you regardless if the request comes via email or phone. Some companies, however, will call you randomly, without warning, and ask to conduct the screening interview at that time. Wow! You may feel unprepared but be afraid to say no! Frankly, these surprise screens typically do not go exceedingly well. A good strategy is, if, while job searching, you receive a call from an unknown number, don't answer it and let it go to voicemail. If it is a screening interview, the caller will identify him or herself, let you know they are interested in talking, and ask you to call back. This strategy allows you to both control the time for the screening and do some preparation!

A screening interview is not to decide whether you get the job. It is to decide whether the company thinks it is worthwhile to send you on to the next step, likely a face-to-face interview. The HR representative conducting the screening is simply trying to make a cursory decision on whether you can do the job.

Qualifying Interviews

Assuming the HR representative deems you acceptable during the screening interview, you will next be notified that the company would like to meet with you in person. Where the screening interview was with someone from HR, the qualifying interview(s) will probably include the hiring manager and maybe members of the team you would be working with. This interview will focus on the "can" and "will" portions of the job. Can you do the job and will you do the job?

The qualifying interview will also be used to determine your cultural fit for the organization. Is there chemistry between you and the company? Will you fit in?

Approval Interviews

You can pretty much be assured that an approval interview will happen in person. If you make it to the approval interview, the hiring manager(s) has already determined that you can do the job, that you would be a good fit, and that there is some chemistry with the organization and its employees. The approval interview is conducted to answer the question, will you do the job?

For entry level positions, there may only be one or two qualifying interviews. For higher level jobs, there may be a series of qualifying interviews. CEO and other executive positions typically involve the most interviews. I have had clients experience five, ten, and even more interviews before a decision is made.

It may help to think of the interview process as a sales process. In this process you are the product or service and the employer is the buyer. Just as a good salesperson does, it is important that you are aware of the employer's needs (the reason they created the job in the first place) and you can effectively communicate how you can help meet those needs.

The biggest mistake job seekers make in interviewing is simple: they don't prepare. Preparation for any interview is crucial to your success. Since many people don't prepare at all or at least don't do it effectively, your preparation can truly make you stand out!

Preparation

What follows is a step-by-step approach to that all-important interview preparation. If you are scheduled for an interview, review this information and put the work in to make sure you are ready.

Answer the question, why are you interested in the job?

Perhaps the company you are interviewing with is one of your target companies. Maybe you have lots of friends that work there. It could be that it's close to home. While those may be legitimate reasons for you to apply for the job, those aren't what the company representatives want to hear. What about this role do you find intriguing? What makes the company one you would be proud to work for? Is this a place you feel you could have a real impact and grow professionally and personally? If so, be prepared to talk about that. Those are the things employers are looking for.

During this preparation, you may find that the company is one that truly does interest you. Or you may find that it really doesn't. Either way, the process has been helpful.

Compare the job posting/description to your resume and cover letter.

Hopefully, you tailored your resume to this position. If so, make sure to review the version of your resume that you used in the application process so you are ready to talk about any of the items on there during the interview. You may consider building a word cloud (see Chapter 11) to help identify the keywords and concepts likely to be mentioned.

If you used the T-format cover letter, reread that document and be sure you can articulate the reasons you included there to show that you are a good fit for the position.

Review your key skills.

Getting a job today is about skills. Companies will talk about culture and fit, but decisions are mostly made on the basis of the skills and experience (and results) you bring to the organization. Make sure that you can show how your core competencies are aligned with the job you are targeting.

In addition to being able to effectively communicate your key skills as they relate to the role, make a list of additional skills you may possess that are not necessarily in the job posting/description, but could be useful in the position. In the interview, the chance will probably arise for you to point out these additional benefits of hiring you for the position.

Every job will require transferable skills, those skills that you learned elsewhere but will come in handy in any position. Make sure you are aware of your transferable skills and be ready to show how they will help you in your role at the company. Some call these your "employability" skills. These are skills such as:

1. Communication skills
2. Teamwork
3. Analytical and problem-solving skills
4. Interpersonal effectiveness
5. Computer and technical literacy
6. Leadership and management skills
7. Learning skills
8. Reading comprehension
9. Math proficiency
10. Strong work ethic

Get your references ready.

While the most common time a prospective employer will ask for your references is near the end of the process, once they have identified you as one of – or the – leading candidates, sometimes that request will come much earlier. Consequently, you should be ready at any time.

In fact, a common question used in interviews is to ask what others think of you or what others would say of you. That's a great invitation to pull out your references and hand them over!

When you prepare your references, you should make sure you do some very important things. First, contact your references to get their permission and also to understand what they are likely to tell someone who calls to check on you. Know what they will say!

Second, a powerful strategy involving references is to ask them to send you a quote about you ahead of time. Then, under each reference's name and contact information on your reference sheet, put their particular quote. Sometimes employers will not even check references since they already know what the reference will say about you. Plus, this is yet another way to differentiate yourself from the pack of applicants.

Research the company.

Employers are most impressed by candidates who have taken the time to learn about the company with which they are interviewing. Surprisingly, many don't bother to perform this important step in the preparation process.

With the proliferation of social media, the opportunity to research a company has never been better or easier. These are some great sources to start with but by no means are they the only ones.

One sure way to impress the interviewer and to demonstrate that you have done your homework is to learn and use the terminology of the company. Do they have acronyms for their computer systems and departments? Are there products unique to the industry? By spending a little time talking to other employees and even customers and vendors, you can pick up substantial information that will be useful in the interview.

The Employer's Website

Companies put tons of information about themselves on their website, waiting for you to look at it! Most sites will have an "about the company" section that will offer a great, brief overview of the organization. You will probably find a section on the leadership of the organization. Look at the people in charge. Do you have things in common? Have they been there very long? Learn the company's mission/vision and be ready to explain how you can help them attain that goal.

Digging a bit deeper on most company sites will yield additional information, such as recent press releases (telling you the things they are most proud of and the changes they are making), copies of past annual reports (for public companies), and even transcripts or recordings of investor phone conferences.

LinkedIn and Facebook

No company worth its salt would be caught dead without a LinkedIn page and a Facebook page. Some are more active than others, but be sure to look at each to see what they have taken time to post and share.

Google

Google the company and select the "news" option near the top of the Google homepage. This will provide lots of articles about the company and the people that work there. Scanning a few of these articles will give you an idea of who they are, what they do, and where they are going.

Glassdoor.com

Glassdoor.com has information on most companies in the United States. Some smaller ones will not be represented. Glassdoor has information on salaries, the typical employment experience, and might even include the company's favorite standard interview questions. Because Glassdoor.com is an open forum, you will probably find reviews from current and past employees which can be quite insightful. However, you should take these with a grain of salt since the person posting the review may have a disagreement with his boss or perhaps was disciplined for being late to work too often. The review will simply talk about how unfairly they were treated while conveniently leaving out their role in the dispute.

Salary.com

Salary.com is the leader in providing free information about salaries for hundreds of different positions. It can be a valuable source for determining the likely range of compensation for a given job and should definitely be consulted before the subject comes up in an interview. However, just because a salary is listed on Salary.com does not mean that the company you are talking to will be offering compensation within that range.

Library

Most public libraries offer free access to various business databases that can be used to research companies you are interested in. A quick visit to the reference librarian will steer you in the right direction for your particular library.

Be ready to talk about salary.

After consulting sources such as Glassdoor.com and Salary. com, prepare yourself for the salary discussion when and if it comes up. Many interviewees hem and haw at the questions. If you are confident in your answer, you will stand out in a positive way.

Although having the salary discussion can be nerve-wracking, some serious consideration ahead of time will prepare you with a confident answer. An acceptable range is a perfectly reasonable answer, although be aware that the company, should it make an offer, will tend toward the low end of that range. So make sure your acceptable number is nearer the bottom.

In addition, it will be helpful for you to have a minimum figure in mind. If you wouldn't accept the position for less than, say, $50,000, be prepared to say that. There is no reason for you to lead the company down the path knowing that you are not going to accept the job. That's not fair to you or them.

One last note on salary. You may have been required to put an expected salary on the application when you applied for the job. Be sure that whatever you say you want now is consistent with that number!

The Leave-Behind

For any in-person interview, you should plan to take a set of folders with you. Prepare enough copies so that each of the interviewers will receive one plus one extra. Often an additional person you weren't expecting will be interviewing you and you need to be prepared.

Even if that doesn't happen, it can be a reference for you during the interview.

The leave-behind folder is another one of these "differentiate yourself from the crowd" moves. You will most likely be the only candidate who takes the time to do this. Leaving it behind for each interviewer will serve as a reminder of who you are as they contemplate the hiring decision. Being the only reminder sitting on the hiring manager's desk while she makes her decision is definitely a good thing!

Ideally, each of these folders should be neutral-colored (or black) and have two pockets. Try to find the type that have the pre-cuts for your business cards. In each folder, include:

1. A copy of your resume
2. A copy of your cover letter (in the T-format)
3. Your marketing profile
4. A print out of your LinkedIn profile
5. A business card
6. Your portfolio

Be certain you have a nice, professional looking portfolio to carry with you to the interview. The type with three rings in the center is ideal as it allows you to use tabs to find information quickly during the interview. Inside include:

1. Twenty business cards
2. Five or more copies of your resume
3. Pens
4. Thank you notes and envelopes
5. "Forever" stamps (in case postal rates change)
6. A calendar or your smartphone
7. A tablet to take notes
8. A completed copy of the application form
9. Examples of your work documents

10. Copies of documents and articles you wrote such as reports and white papers
11. Samples of presentations, business plans, social media blogs, etc.
12. Copy of past work such as pictures, flow charts, and news clippings
13. Certifications and certificates
14. Licenses
15. Military records
16. Volunteer/Community service
17. Thank you notes and awards

Joe developed what he called a "Brag Book," containing his resume, highlights from his career, letters of recommendation, and references, among other things. He made sure he had one prepared, and personalized, for each one of his interviewers. The feedback Joe received from the person who hired him was that his being so well prepared was a deciding factor in offering him the position.

The Interview Itself

A screening interview is typically on the phone, although the company may request that you conduct the interview online, using media such as Skype or Facetime. If that is the case, or if the interview is face-to-face at the company's offices, your appearance is vitally important. Some researchers say that HR professionals and hiring managers make snap decisions about your fitness for a position in the first few seconds, based solely on your appearance.

The first issue you will have to deal with is the proper dress. This decision used to be an easy one, as all interviewees were expected to arrive in suits and ties for men, or professional business suits for women. After all, no one would have come to work in anything else! Today, however, the acceptable attire in the workplace runs the gamut from the venerable suit and tie to shorts and t-shirts, depending on the type of business and the culture the company is trying to create and maintain.

Under no circumstances should you plan to attend a face-to-face interview in attire less than business casual. This is the case even if the people who already work there are more casual. You always want to dress at least a step above what you might wear on a daily basis. For men, this means jackets are optional but no ties. For women, no jeans, sandals, or short skirts.

The easiest way to choose the appropriate dress for your interview is to ask the person when the request for the interview is made. Confirming the desired attire is completely acceptable and will show your consideration for the interviewers as well. A simple note confirming the interview place and time and asking for the name(s) of the interviewer(s) and if you should wear professional or business casual attire should be part of your standard regimen.

Regardless of the direction you take, business or business casual, you should follow some basic rules to ensure you make a good first impression and are not ruled out before you even have a chance to sell the company on your assets. These include:

- Dressing conservatively (avoid flashy patterns or trendy clothing)
- If needed, a solid color or muted pattern sport coat or jacket
- Hair and fingernails trimmed and cleaned
- No heavy cologne/fragrance – some people are also allergic
- No chewing gum, cigarettes (or cigarette smell on clothing)
- Polished shoes
- For men, make sure to shave and/or trim facial hair, wear dark shoes and socks, remove earrings, excess jewelry, and cover tattoos where possible.
- For women, avoid heavy makeup (a more natural look is best), keep jewelry to a minimum, and avoid extremely high heels and long fingernails.

Arrival

Even before the time you arrive for your interview, you are likely being scrutinized. It is a highly common practice for an interviewer to quiz others who interacted with a candidate prior to or after the interview to get feedback on the person when the candidate is not "on" in the interview room.

Do not arrive at the appointed time. You should be there at least ten to fifteen minutes early. You will likely still be asked in at the appointed time so be aware that you will likely have to wait for a few minutes. Arriving early shows consideration for the time of the interviewers.

Upon your arrival and check in, introduce yourself to the receptionist and shake hands. Don't simply say you are there to meet with John Smith at 11:00. That receptionist just may help to sway the decision of the hiring manager!

Take the time before you are called in to observe the space. Are there awards and other things the company is proud of on the walls? What does the workspace look like? Are people moving about busily? These are all cues that you might be able to use to your advantage in the interview.

It is said that first impressions are lasting impressions. Be likeable, friendly, and approachable. Smile. Give a firm handshake to everyone you meet while making eye contact. Show your enthusiasm for the position. Sit forward in your chair and use the interviewer's name when appropriate.

Remember, if you are being interviewed, the decision has already been made that you are a viable candidate and that you meet the skill requirements. The person they will hire is the one that impresses them and that they like!

Do not arrive at the appointed time. You should be there at least ten to fifteen minutes early.

Searching for a job is a long process for many people and it is quite easy to get discouraged. But it is imperative that you do not project that discouragement or any desperation you may feel to the interviewer. You may be feeling that you NEED this job. You may even feel as though you HAVE to have it to survive. But that type of attitude, if communicated to the interviewer, is a sure-fire way to turn them off and incline them to give the position to another, more positive candidate.

Project confidence! Never start the interview by saying that you want or need the job. You are interviewing them as much as they are interviewing you!

There are some tricks and techniques you can employ to make sure you project that confident manner during the interview. Many people will stand before a mirror prior to the interview, hands on hips (a power pose) and talk to themselves about how they are the perfect pick for this position. Think of your past successes and envision yourself creating even bigger wins for this employer!

Some other considerations:

- Avoid excess caffeine. If your body is not used to a large amount, it can make you jittery, your hands shaky, and may imply that you are overly nervous.
- Decline refreshments except for water. Many companies will offer you a drink. Judgments can be made on choices of sodas, etc., plus spilling most drinks can be a disaster in an interview. Water is a safe bet.
- Be courteous to everyone. Remember, the main interviewer will probably be asking for opinions about you and you have no idea who might be the ultimate decision maker!
- Don't smoke prior to or during the interview. Today, fewer and fewer people are smokers and more and more are turned off by the habit. Even though you may really need a cigarette, try not to indulge immediately before the interview as the smell lingers on you – even though you don't think it does.
- Don't discuss sex, race, national origin, religion, or age. Interviewers should not bring these topics up and you shouldn't open that door by mentioning them yourself.

- Do not bring up salary discussions, benefits, or vacation time too early in the process. Those are for the offer phase after you have won them over in the interviews.

Interview Questions

Virtually every interview today is based on a technique called behavioral interviewing. While you will be asked some generic questions about your skills and background, the most important questions will probably be phrased in ways to determine how you will respond in a given situation. These behavioral questions usually start with something like "Tell me about a time when...." The nice thing about these questions is that they are a direct invitation to show off.

When asked a question by the interviewer you should be brief. Most people have an attention span that is much shorter than expected, typically only about ninety seconds or less. Give a brief and direct answer to the question asked, then allow them to ask for more information in follow up questions if desired.

Once you have answered a question, stop talking. Silence is awkward for many people, but perfectly acceptable in an interview. The interviewer may be thinking of the next question or checking her notes. That is not an invitation for you to ramble or go off on some tangent. Sit quietly and await the next inquiry.

Listening is a key skill in an interview. The best interviews are often the ones in which you talk the least. Be present when the interviewer is talking and pay attention to the question being asked. If the question is unclear, ask clarifying questions. Practice "active listening" in which you paraphrase questions to assure you understand them. And, again, maintain eye contact.

Your parents likely told you over and over again not to brag. While that is generally good advice in life, you have to relax that rule a bit in a job interview. If you don't sell yourself to the interviewer, no one will and you won't get the job. Don't be afraid to take credit where credit is due. Make sure you say "I" when you did something or caused something to be done. While the tendency is to spread credit around by saying "we," you are the only one being considered for the job.

Don't exaggerate or give too much information. Keep your answers relevant to the question. Sales people know that they can talk themselves out of a sale. That is the same in an interview. Once the interviewer has the information requested, there is nothing more you can say to enhance your chances. You can only say something to distract from the answer you gave. And exaggerations are usually discovered, making you appear untrustworthy.

Be specific. Use the STAR (Situation, Task, Action, Result) model when answering questions. Be ready with plenty of examples of how you did things and what the impact was. The more you can connect the dots between your actions and the success for the company, the more powerful and memorable the answer.

Avoid emotional responses. Keep your answers businesslike. Some interviewers may try to challenge you in the interview. If that is the case, simply present your answers and stop. The winner in an argument is probably not going to get hired.

The "kick off" question

Chances are your interview (screening or face-to-face) will start with the same question every time: "Tell me about yourself." This can be a difficult question on several planes since you are pre-programmed not to brag on and on about yourself and you are probably unsure of what the interviewer is actually looking for. You don't necessarily want to say something that will rule you out before you even get past the first question.

This question is really a great opportunity for you to convey what you want them to know, to present your personal brand. Before the interview, prepare a sixty second infomercial about yourself, telling about your brand and your biggest accomplishments (review Chapter 8). In essence, make your pitch that you are the right fit for this position.

Including an unusual fact about your career or even an outside interest will also humanize you during this answer. It will often make you much more memorable and even lead to some "off the record" discussion, all of which make you more likable.

The following is a template that you might use to construct your answer to this common interview question:

1. *Address the target position*

   I am a <functional job title> experienced in <industry, area>. Some of my key strengths are <two to three key strengths that you have identified>.

   You might also include a few personal traits such as, "I am an analytical, detail-oriented project engineer...."

2. *Most recent position*

   Most recently, I was <job title> at <company>, where I handled <key areas of responsibility>. <List a few accomplishments from that job.>

3. *Career history*

   Give a brief summary of the last couple jobs you held. DO NOT include more than two or three and only if they are relevant. Highlight the key themes and impact you have had including a couple accomplishments as examples.

4. *Reason for leaving*

   The interviewer may ask you why you left your last position. By bringing it up first, you are controlling the narrative and diffusing any awkward discussion later in the interview. Be sure to give a business reason for leaving your last job. Be brief. Be positive. Be honest.

5. *Future*

Finally, list a couple of goals you have for the future such as classes you would like to take, positions you aspire to, certifications you want to achieve.

STAR Stories

The best response to behavioral interviewing questions ("Tell me about a time when...") is the STAR story. As mentioned earlier, STAR stands for situation, task, action, and result. Every answer will include each of these elements. (Some people refer to these as SOAR stories: situation, opportunity, action, and result. In practice, they are the same.)

For example, if an interviewer were to ask you to talk about a time when you faced a very difficult deadline, your answer might be something like this:

"When I was a product development engineer with Motorola, a colleague abruptly left and I was assigned his project due to go to market in three months. After getting up to speed, I realized the project was actually well behind schedule for the launch date. (Situation) I had to come up with a way to get it back on track quickly. (Task) I immediately brought the team together and we agreed that we would meet the original timeline and reworked the project plan to establish deadlines that would be challenging but doable. (Action) I was able to push the team and help them meet the original launch date and we introduced the product in time for the Fall trade show." (Result)

> **The best response to behavioral interviewing questions is the STAR story.**

In order to successfully formulate a STAR story in answer to a behavioral question, it may be helpful to quickly to determine a few things. These include:

Is this a question that is designed to see if you are a good match for the position? Some questions will help you demonstrate how good a match you will be for the job. These will typically include inquiries about specific skills and where you have used those skills. If that is the case, be sure to highlight your successful usage of those skills, but also take the opportunity to comment about how well you worked with others and teams to show you would fit in the culture of the new workplace.

Is there really a question behind that question? Sometimes the interviewer is asking a sort of indirect question rather than directly asking the question she wants to know. These may not be couched in the behavioral language, but instead may be a statement. For example, an interviewer might say, "You appear overqualified for this position." In this case, the interviewer is not really telling you that you aren't right for the job. She is simply looking for you to defend that you are the best option AND to convince her of some unasked issues such as, "Will you be bored? Will you only stay for a short time?"

In your answer, try your best to address not only the asked question but the underlying issues as well. You might point out that your skills and strengths align very well with the position (answering what was asked). Then add that you are very interested in the company (i.e., likely to stay) and see this role as one that may evolve over time ("I won't be bored").

Tough Questions

Sometimes you may be hit with an especially tough question, one that is focused on a negative aspect. It may be about why you have switched jobs frequently in the past, or about a gap in employment. Or the interviewer may want more information about a perceived weakness.

Being honest is paramount in an interview, but there is a strategy you might employ in the face of a tough question to help answer it positively. This is known as the "sandwich" model.

The sandwich model consists of three layers, two pieces of

"bread" and one of "meat." The first, or top layer is the answer with a positive comment. The best response is to try to highlight a related strength. For example, if the interviewer were to ask why you were let go from your last position, be honest about the circumstances (It clearly wasn't a good fit. Don't give too many details if possible). Discuss your optimism and resilience in the face of this setback and how you viewed it positively.

The second layer of the sandwich model is to respond directly to the negative question. Talk about how that event has given you the opportunity to pursue something you are much more passionate about, such as this position.

The third, or final layer, is to close with a positive observation. Take the opportunity to reflect on how you have overcome or deflected that weakness. "I gained valuable experience in that position and although it didn't end as I expected, I know that I can now use those new assets to help in other roles such as this one."

Nonverbal Communication

As important as preparation is for your interview, it is not the only thing you should be concerned about. Dr. Albert Mehrabian, author of *Silent Messages*, conducted several studies on nonverbal communication. He found that 7% of any message is conveyed through words, 38% through certain vocal elements, and 55% through nonverbal elements (facial expressions, gestures, posture, etc). This means that your posture and gestures may be more important than your answers. It's not just about what you say but how you say it.

Be aware of how you are communicating to others. Keep your tone business-like, but be sure to show positive energy about areas that interest you and about the company and position.

Body Language – Do's

- Shake hands firmly and smile!
- Lean forward slightly to indicate interest

- Wait to talk until the other person is finished
- Nod to show your understanding
- Wear glasses if needed
- Keep your hands folded in front of you or on the table
- Use subtle gestures when speaking
- Mirror the interviewer's behavior
- Refer to your resume when needed
- Keep your feet still
- Stand and walk tall
- Relax!

Body Language – Don'ts

- Staring
- Shifting your eyes
- Closing your eyes
- Smiling continuously and inappropriately
- Wrinkling your brow
- Interrupting others
- Nodding rapidly
- Putting hands in your mouth/biting your nails
- Nervous coughing
- Dark glasses
- Looking over your glasses at others
- Leaning too far back
- Folding arms across your chest
- Clasping hands behind your head
- Slouching
- Acting hurried

Your Turn to Ask Questions

In any interview, you will most likely be asked if you have any questions, usually at the end of the interview. Your answer should always be yes!

An interview is a dialogue and it is a chance for them to learn about you and for you to learn about them. You should always be ready with at least a few questions to ask the interviewer, as this is a demonstration of your level of interest in the company and the position as well as a way to show your research.

Your questions should address the elements that are important to you. Write them out prior to the interview and don't be afraid to refer to them when the time comes.

Some examples of questions are:

- What are the company's goal for this position?
- What do you see as success in this role?
- Where do you think this position will go in the next two or three years?
- What does the department (or company) hope to achieve in the next two to three years?
- What would be the initial top three objectives that you would like me to achieve in the job?
- I saw some information on your website about…. Can you tell me more about that?
- How long have you been with the company?
- What do you like most about working here?
- How would you describe the culture of the organization?
- Who will I be working with?
- Who will I report to?
- What will my core responsibilities be – most critical to the role?
- What are the elements that maybe didn't make the posted job description?
- What are your expectations of me in the first ninety days?

The Closer

Regardless of the type of interview, you should get in the habit of closing the interview with a question for the interviewer: "Based on our conversation today, do you have any concerns about my ability to do the job?"

This type of statement, in the sales realm, is known as a "trial close" and it is used to uncover and handle any objections the interviewer may have to your candidacy. This gives you the chance to address any issues immediately.

If the response is positive and there are no issues to deal with, ask what, when, and where. What are the next steps in the process and the timeframe? When is a good time for me to contact you to follow up? Who is my best point of contact from here?

Follow Up

During the interview or immediately thereafter, be sure you record the names and job titles of the person or people you met with. Securing business cards is the easiest way to do this. Also make a few notes about the key points of the job and the interview. Note any questions that you feel didn't go particularly well.

Then, as quickly as possible, send thank you notes to everyone you interviewed with. In most cases, a handwritten thank you mailed to the interviewer will have the biggest impact and is most likely to set you apart from others being interviewed. However, for some positions, such as IT, email may be the preferred method of communication (review Chapter 14). In your note, thank the interviewer for their time and attention, mention something from the interview (perhaps the interviewer mentioned that they are short-staffed and anxious to fill the position), and tell him you are looking forward to continuing in the process.

Unfortunately, many hiring managers will tell you a timeframe but then get busy with other priorities and you do not hear back as promised. This is not necessarily a reflection on you or your candidacy for the position. So plan to follow up in a timely fashion.

If you did not nail down a timeframe, in no more than two weeks, call the interviewer or hiring manager. You may get their voicemail, but either way, simply reiterate your interest in the position and offer to provide any other information that might help them in the decision-making process. If you do not receive a response, in another week or two, follow up with an email saying the same thing.

We saw from the research earlier in this book that being proactive in follow up is one of the most crucial and successful techniques that a job seeker can use to get a position. Yet most are scared of appearing to be a pest and ruining the possibility of getting the job. But remember, as we said before, if they like you, following up won't change that. And if they don't like you, following up won't change that either!

As much as we might enjoy a job, getting paid is really why we work! So salary is an important element of the job offer when it comes. It can also be one of the toughest and most stressful.

Nathan was interviewing as a high-level data analyst when the C-level executive he was interviewing with surprisingly offered him a salary figure. Caught off-guard, Nathan responded, "Sounds good to me," thinking it was around his salary at his previous position. After the interview, Nathan began wondering what he had just agreed to. Was it really reflective of his worth to the organization? Nathan and his career coach reviewed resources to research salary ranges both nationally and regionally and talked through ways to bring the conversation back up before accepting any offer.

After the research, Nathan found that the appropriate compensation range for the position was above the figure he had been "offered" earlier. In his next interview, he proposed a new compensation, 15% higher than what was discussed the week before and backed it up with key facts from his research and pointed out that the role had some clear expectations for growth and increased strategic value. Nathan's proposal was accepted and he started work two weeks later – at the higher salary.

CHAPTER SIXTEEN

Tracking Your Progress

The fact that online job submissions make the process of applying for a job much easier creates an issue: many job seekers have difficulty remembering which jobs they have applied for!

Now that might not seem like much of a problem, but if you are following the process this book outlines, it certainly should be! After all, you have customized your resume for each position and, should you be contacted for an interview, it is crucial that you have a copy of that resume available to answer questions and relate applicable STAR stories to highlight your accomplishments.

Also, many online application systems require a registration process to apply. This means that you will have to create a username and password for each submission. Using the same username is certainly not a problem and consistently using your first and last names combined in one word (janestephonowoski or stevesimpson) is an option. A first letter and last name are also common (jstephonowski, ssimpson). If you have a common name, the system may force you to be slightly more creative, possibly suggesting you add a number (such as a graduation year) to ensure the uniqueness of your username.

The real trick is often the password. Unfortunately and ill-advisedly, many people tend to use the same password for every application and website. Identity thieves can more easily wreak havoc on your entire life if they happen to discover your login info from one site and begin applying it to others, such as bank accounts. To make matters worse, research has shown year after year that most of us also tend to choose unbelievably rudimentary and easy to guess passwords. The most popular password continues to be "password," with a close runner up of 123456. Consequently, these are the ones hackers begin with when trying to guess login information.

There are several free sites that will generate completely random and difficult to hack passwords on the Internet. Creating a unique password for each application site is certainly advisable, but I realize that creating a different one every time is not easy and those generated randomly are less than memorable.

The solution is to track your application submissions, including the password you used for the site. (Of course, if you forget the password, sites regularly have protocols you can employ to recover and reset your password, but having it to begin with is much easier).

Another common issue is one of minimum salary. The majority of application sites these days will ask you for a minimum acceptable salary or a range which you expect. As you apply for more and more jobs, you will often find yourself adjusting that number for each position. If you apply for a claims adjuster position at a company well-known in the industry for being a difficult place to work, you may say on your application that you expect at least $75,000. On the other hand, if an interesting position comes up at your dream company, or at a place with other compensation available such as tuition assistance, you may want that job enough that you are willing to work there for $60,000. When and if you get an interview, the subject of compensation will arise at some point and you will not make a favorable impression if you can't remember what you requested or give the wrong number.

Again, the solution is to track your submissions including your salary requirement.

A final reason to track your activity is to make sure you remember the name(s) of the person(s) who either referred you to the company or is a contact(s) that can be leveraged during the process. Keeping in touch and following up with those contacts is easier with a plan.

I have seen job seekers build their own tracking spreadsheets, some with just a few fields and some with many fields running onto extra pages. I have noticed that those in technical professions, such as engineers, scientists, and actuaries, often create very large spreadsheets for this task! I have included a fairly basic version that should fit the bill below. However, feel free to build your own to fit your needs. There is no right or wrong way to complete this task in your job search. There is only the way that works best for you.

In that vein, here are some potential fields you should consider:

1. *Date of Application*

   You should always include the date of application and I recommend that it be one of (if not) the first fields in your tracking sheet. So much of your plan to find your next job revolves around your proactivity, and ensuring that you follow up in a timely manner is crucial. That activity keys off the date you submitted your application, so make sure that information is easy to find.

   Making the date of application the first field makes it easiest to add to the list. You are always simply adding to the end as you apply to other positions. The most relevant jobs (your hottest prospects) are commonly the most recent, so grouping these together makes it easier to watch and act on them as needed. (With Excel, you are also able to sort by columns and can always perform a sort by "date of application" if needed.)

2. *Job Title*

   The title of the position is obviously important and should be included in your tracking efforts. While you may have been a CFO at your last company, other companies may have similar positions with different names (i.e. controller or senior financial executive). Different sized companies may also offer similar opportunities at different levels than you were at previously. A VP spot at a small company may be comparable to a director at a larger organization.

3. *Job Description*

The job description trips up many job seekers when it comes to interview time. It is always a good idea to refresh your memory regarding the job description prior to any interview, or even a phone screen. This information is vital so that you are certain to address the pertinent issues the company is looking to solve. As each job description is unique, keeping all of them straight is nearly impossible.

Here's the rub: often companies will remove the job description before starting interviews! Once they have an adequate candidate pool, they take down the posting. And when you get an interview request and revisit the website, the description is nowhere to be found!

Cutting and pasting the entire job description in a spreadsheet is pretty inefficient. However, you can save a copy in an electronic file folder with a link on your spreadsheet or, if you are a little less high-tech, keeping all of them in a paper folder works well, too.

4. *Website*

A company's website is usually a treasure trove of preparatory information for a job interview. You can learn about the mission and vision, the history, what they are most proud of, the location of offices, and even names, titles, and background for the leadership. You may be able to learn about the person you will be interviewing with! Including the link to the company website in your tracking sheet saves time in finding the site again when needed.

5. Contacts

We have learned time and again that the best route to a new position is through networking within the company. The chapters on networking and on LinkedIn will be invaluable here. List each of the contacts that you have at the company, including contact information and the extent of their influence. For example, you might include John Smith at johnsmith@gmail.com, a phone number, and a note that John is friends with the CIO at the company. Including a field chronicling communications with the person allows you to know when and how to follow up.

6. *Deadline*

Some positions include deadlines for applications after which the posting will be removed and the process will move forward. Some job seekers find it helpful to have that information so they can check in and follow up once the process is closed and "make their case."

7. *Process Stage*

While we as job seekers would love for the process to be uniform and predictable and, most importantly, quick, that just isn't the case. I have seen people who apply for jobs receive a call within the hour. Others take weeks or even months. So a field indicating where you are in the process can be helpful, especially if you are lucky enough to have several "fish" on the line simultaneously. You can use terminology as simple as "applied," "phone screen," "interviewing," "waiting on decision," and "offer pending." The wording is not important. Use what works for you.

Exercise:

By now you should have developed the tools and techniques that will lead you to your next job. Every piece of the worksheet you were introduced to at the beginning of the book are now in place.

Pull that worksheet back out. Make it your daily guide to activity and your overall roadmap to job search success.

You are accountable to yourself in this process. No one else wants you to get that job more than you. This worksheet and the things you have learned are the gas in your job search engine!

CHAPTER SEVENTEEN
Using A Career Coach

One of the major issues facing many job seekers surrounds the feeling of isolation that you may experience as you embark on and proceed through your job search. Many people struggle with such emotions after working in a corporate environment where friendships are developed, ideas shared, and relationships formed. Suddenly, you find yourself on your own, wondering if what you are doing is working as you often meet silence and delays from your contacts and target companies.

While job search groups such as TNG can certainly help with that feeling of isolation and the doubts that naturally creep in, many job seekers also choose to work with a career coach. Working with a career coach can, in effect, provide you a partner to help guide you through a very foreign process, encourage you, hold you accountable, and, most of all, serve as an additional support system for you to bounce ideas off and to hear different perspectives from.

What is Career Coaching?

As the name "career coach" implies, your career coach serves as your job search "coach." Put simply, a coach exists to help a person – athlete or job seeker – focus on that person's goals. In fact, one of the most concise and eloquent definitions of a coach comes from Master Coach Cathy Liska:

"A coach helps empower you to become more, or achieve more, than you could on your own."

Coaching as an industry is rapidly growing in its own right. Today there are career coaches, executive coaches, leadership coaches, health coaches, fitness/exercise coaches, and even life coaches. The list doesn't stop there!

Many job seekers also choose to work with a career coach.

An effective career coach helps you uncover or rediscover yourself, unearthing new insights and perspectives involving these areas:

- Your innate character traits
- Attributes you demonstrate in the workplace
- Your areas of strength
- Your skills
- Your value to prospective employers and clients.

A career coach will also help you set objectives for the process. These will likely include things such as:

- Understanding your core strengths, skills, and value (and those transferable skills)
- Determining your target career options
- Clearly articulating your key value and message (your "personal brand")
- Representing your "brand" in various forms (targeted resumes, cover letters, LinkedIn and other social media, verbal networking, etc.)
- Developing and executing an effective targeting and networking strategy toward your target career(s)
- Interview preparation, debrief, and employment negotiations

In short, a career coach engages with you to help you personally develop and apply the very disciplines and principles you are discovering in this book!

A job search coach isn't always about finding a new job or a new place to work. A good coach can also help improve the job you have as well as position you for future jobs inside or outside your current company, as Gretchen found out.

Gretchen had fifteen years with her marketing company, working as a project manager for the last several years. Although Gretchen didn't dislike her job or the organization, she felt frustrated and somewhat bored in her role and wanted to do more "advanced" work. And, frankly, she just didn't feel like her company "got" her. She knew they didn't realize her full potential.

Gretchen worked with Mike Johnson to assess her core strengths and transferable skills and to identify what activities she was most interested in. They found she was very effective working with teams and using her intuition to conceive new approaches, options, and impacts. They used that information to update her resume and begin thinking through the kind of organizations she wanted to pursue.

Through the process, Gretchen reported some "aha" moments, including:

- She really wanted to do more strategic-level marketing work - designing campaigns, setting direction, developing messaging, implementation beyond and between events, and more.

- She discovered that her own company had a strategic marketing role that looked like a good fit for her (though it was out of state and would require her to move with her family).

Armed with her new discoveries, Gretchen met with her manager and received positive feedback during the discussion. She even received approval to move forward with two prototype projects. Over the next three months, Gretchen balanced her time between her current role and implementing these projects. The result was significant: one saved the firm over $120,000; the other yielded more tangible sales leads.

Soon, news of her success reached higher in the organization and the executives asked her to write up both as case studies which were then promoted across her site and division. At her annual evaluation, her manager recognized her interests and accomplishments and helped Gretchen negotiate her way into a new position as Marketing Event Strategist.

Gretchen found her dream position all without having to switch companies!

Gretchen credits coaching with the successes she experienced. According to Gretchen, coaching "set me on a path to accomplish my career goals, and I had that "aha" moment when we discovered what exactly those goals were."

The Role of the Coach

Your career coach will serve as a strategic partner to assist you in defining or clarifying your career strategy. Your coach will also serve as an accountability partner, helping you build momentum through the day-to-day activities and distractions of life. Your coach will help you create a vision of future possibilities, brainstorm options, act as a sounding board for ideas, examine obstacles or barriers AND ways to overcome them, develop action plans, and checkpoint your progress.

To illustrate how working with a career coach might work for you, consider these three different situations in which a coach might be helpful.

The Coach as a Mirror

When you get ready to start your day, you usually look in the bathroom mirror before leaving the house. Why? Because the mirror gives you an objective reflection of yourself that you otherwise would not see! How does your hair look? Are you happy with your makeup? Do you have remnants of breakfast stuck in your teeth? Coaching serves as your career mirror, helping you examine yourself, both to affirm you and to identify things that might be very evident to others but not to yourself. How does the coach do this? A coach asks questions – lots of questions. Often these questions can be penetrating and uncomfortable. But this intense questioning is also quite effective.

As a modern society, we tend to be prone to short-term, tactical, and practical solutions, and concerned about the urgent needs of our family and friends. We tend not to delve very deeply when examining ourselves (it was Plato quoting Socrates thousands of years ago when he said, "The unexamined life is not worth living." Still very true today!).

Coaching helps you affirm who you are as a whole person. It will also often discover insights about yourself that are fresh or may have been forgotten or left behind in the normal ebb and flow of life. When was the last time you had an "aha" moment about who you are, about your genetic "wiring," or what motivates or drives you? What was the last project or activity you engaged in that got you excited? Your career coach helps bring those things to light.

The Coach as a Compass

Many boys are involved in the Boys Scouts and I was no exception. As a Boy Scout, I learned all sorts of practical skills from camping to hiking, canoeing to first aid. The Boy Scouts taught me to enjoy and respect the outdoors. One of the skills I learned during my days with the Scouts is called orienteering. With orienteering, you are given a compass and a map. You determine where it is you want to go, then you *orient* yourself to the direction you need to go. You have a destination and a direction. You use the compass periodically to affirm that you are on the right course.

Career coaching serves a role similar to the compass in

orienteering. Consider this: the compass does not determine the destination or the direction. You do. The compass helps you orient yourself toward your destination and then helps you keep on course. Much like the compass, your coach helps you assess your career goals, assists you in mapping out a strategy, keeps you "on course" towards those goals, and serves as a periodic checkpoint to keep you moving forward.

The Coach as a General Contractor/Consultant

My wife loves HGTV (Home and Garden Television). You may recognize some of the people appearing on HGTV as they have become near household names. Chip and Joanna Gaines on Fixer Upper. The Scott twins on Property Brothers. My wife is intrigued by how the professional contractors on the programs work with a client to understand what they want (their goals – a new house or a renovation – and helping shape a vision of the new environment – removing a well, repurposing a space). You will often hear the contractors ask questions like, "How about this?" or "What can we design together?" or "Will this kitchen meet your needs?"

Much of the value the contractor adds to the project is in assisting the hosts and homeowners to envision new ideas for a remodel or to repurpose an existing space, decorate, or even add finishing touches like landscaping. My wife and I have seen some very neat ideas that she has then used in our home (Although, confidentially, I have to hire out a lot of the work. I'm nowhere near handy enough to do them myself). Often you will see the homeowner right there in the demolition phase of the project, swinging a sledgehammer to knock out a wall or helping with the small details to create the new space.

We can apply that same logic to your career. Are you looking to "relocate" to a new "house" (that is, a new career)? Are you looking to find a "fixer upper" (a place that you can add new skills or take on a new challenge with a larger scope of authority)?

As the general contractor for your job search, the career coach can help you envision your new career "space." Your coach will work with you to determine what that can look like. What role or position do you really want? What core skills do you most want to use in your job? What kind of work environment best matches your preferences and work style?

Next, you and your coach will work together to "scope" a plan – the coach serving as a sounding board (much as the contractor does on HGTV) on the timeframe, what it will take to get it done, and actions to move forward to your target. Much like an invested homeowner, you are right there in the thick working the actions with perspective and some helpful guidance.

You may have noticed another twist to this analogy. Just as the contractor is an expert on the process, not the end result, your career coach will provide the perspective and guidance, giving you the current best practices in different disciplines (like the resume, cover letter, etc). But it's up to you to apply them. An effective career coach will not tell you "this is the career for you." You will determine your destination.

What Coaching Isn't

Coaching can be very valuable as a complement to your job search. Many people credit the work with their career coach with helping them discover the "perfect" career and helping them go get it. Others testify that the work done with a career coach significantly shortened their job search duration. But there are certain things that a career coach is not.

Remember, a career coach may serve other roles informally, such as being a support for you when things seem bleak. But these are not "technically" a part of the career coach process. In addition, your career coach is not:

<u>An athletic coach</u>. Many if not most of us have had some level of experience with coaching through participation in a sport. That may have come from school, a parks program, college, or university. The athletic coach most often played the sport in younger days and has

adapted his or her skills and knowledge of that sport, strategy and tactics, to mentor those being coached.

There are some similarities to the athletic coach. A career coach, like the athletic coach, is motivated by success and will go to great lengths to help people succeed. The athletic coach is driven to get more from people than they realize they had, to help build a vision to improve skills, play and teamwork.

There are differences as well. A career coach is likely not an expert at your target career. That's not the point of career coaching. A coach doesn't have to be an expert in your career. He or she needs to be an expert in the process and disciplines that lead you to that career.

A counselor. Many people have engaged a counselor to help deal with issues from their past. That person helps us understand ourselves and will help us build coping strategies and move forward. And, once again, you will see similarities.

A counselor will seek to understand you and what motivates you, holding regular sessions to keep momentum and accountability. Likewise, your career coach will meet with you regularly, holding you accountable and striving to understand you and your motivations. But a career coach differs in that we start with you as you are today. We don't delve into the past. Your coach will focus on the present, "in the moment," helping you to develop goals and move forward from this point. Career coaches often have credentials for coaching but are usually not equipped to diagnose and treat behavioral issues.

A mentor. If you have been lucky enough to have a mentor in your career, someone who has mastered a skill we strive to master, someone who takes the time to teach us and work together on our success, you know how great that relationship can be!

Just like a mentor, a career coach won't do things for you. Instead, he or she will teach you how to do things for yourself. Like the mentor, the career coach relishes in your success!

But, remember, the learning and application of the skills in your job search are your responsibility. Your coach is a sounding board for you and an accountability partner but, as a rule, will not tell you what to do or which career you should choose. He or she will help you develop options and discover which of these options you feel are the best for you.

A consultant. Businesses love to bring in consultants and you may have worked with some in the past. Typically, a consultant's role is to understand the business, analyze areas such as finance, IT, HR, or operations, but usually the consultant focuses mainly on the processes of the business. The consultant is paid because they have the business experience and information. They are paid not for what they do, but for their opinion and advice.

This is also true for a career coach. A good career coach knows what works well and what doesn't. This will save you from the trial and error process that many new job seekers go through.

The biggest difference, however, is that the career coach is NOT paid for advice and opinions. He or she is paid for asking the right questions, helping you uncover important facts, concepts, ideas and insights. Often these are things you may already know, have forgotten that you know, or don't even realize that you know!

In all of these roles, the key distinction is that the main focus is not the coach – it is YOU!

Benefits of Hiring a Coach

Some people say they don't need a coach to help them. And, frankly, they may be correct. But for others, they will benefit greatly from the services a career coach will provide. That's a decision only you can make. But consider these reasons that a coach may be helpful in your situation.

A career coach can help you facilitate your transition.

By asking the right questions, a career coach will help you uncover and recognize your areas of high potential, the strengths you have and which ones you want to use regularly, how to go about finding your next career, and guiding you to the next step.

A career coach can be your sounding board.

Throughout this book, we have reiterated the importance of networking in finding a job. A career coach will help you bounce networking ideas around. He or she can often help you identify the most effective points of contact at a target company and put together a plan to successfully approach those identified potential connections. You can then debrief your activities and improve on the ones that worked and avoid the ones that didn't. A career coach will also likely help you prepare for interviews, assisting in developing great answers to common questions and easing the anxiety you may feel. Remember the old saying, "Success is 90% preparation and 10% inspiration!"

A career coach can be a helpful critic.

No one likes to hear criticism. But it is much better to find out about any behaviors you exhibit that may derail your job search before they appear in a job interview. A good career coach will honestly and constructively help you identify behaviors that you may not be aware of. And, best of all, the coach can help you find ways to change them!

A career coach can offer perspective.

There is no way you can be objective when dealing with personal issues. You are yourself, after all! A career coach can provide that needed objectivity, plus he or she can have experience from his or her own life that may help you understand what you want, what you are getting into, and how to get it!

A career coach can serve as a catalyst – and a professional nag.

A career coach will work to empower you, as a strategic partner, sounding board, and accountability partner. A career coach can keep you going when the going gets tough. Your coach may also get on your nerves when you feel like he or she is nagging you. But do you know why people nag? Because it works.

Does Professional Coaching Really Work?

For job seekers, money is often a concern. Even if you have thousands in the bank, the prospect of being unemployed for some undetermined period can instill fear every time a bill appears in the mail. Of course, career coaching isn't free, so you may understandably be wondering if it is worth the money. Only you know the ultimate answer to that question. But I can share with you details on a study that was conducted a few years ago to determine if there really is a return on investment when engaging a career coach. While this study involved executive coaching rather than career coaching, the findings are relevant to both.

In the study, two business professionals studied the impact of executive coaching on thirty-one managers in a U.S. city health agency. The study was conducted in two phases.

In phase one, all managers participated in a three-day, classroom-style training workshop that included a variety of interactive activities focused on their work roles. The participants rated the workshop very highly on all quantitative and qualitative measures. The authors of the study determined that their training intervention increased manager productivity by 22% (That's quite impressive by training standards).

In phase two, the managers participated in an eight-week, one-on-one coaching program that involved coaching tailored to their roles at the agency. The post-training coaching included goal setting, collaborative problem solving, practice, feedback, supervisory involvement, evaluation of end results, and a public presentation. The managers continued to meet with their coaches for one hour each week over a two-month period.

By adding the one-on-one coaching intervention after the training, the managers' productivity was increased by 88%!

In a nutshell, your career coach can help you become more impactful and productive in applying and adapting the various tools and techniques you learn in this book!

What to Look for in a Coach

As in any industry, not all career coaches are created equally. There is no legal requirement that a career coach complete a training program and there is no licensing authority like there is for realtors and insurance agents. In short, anyone who wants to call himself or herself a career coach can.

Consequently, the onus is on you to make sure that the career coach you engage is both competent and the right person to help you reach your career goals as efficiently and effectively as possible.

The following are some criteria you should consider before engaging a career coach.

Methodology: Does the coach have a clear methodology or process? Can he or she articulate it to you?

Experience and results: What is the coach's background? What level of experience does he or she have in career coaching? Is the process he or she employs proven to work? What is the coach's track record? What do past and present clients say about the coach's services?

Commitment to Ethical Standards: Does the coach recognize and adhere to ethical standards for coaching? (An example is the International Coach Federations' published Core Competencies for Coaches). Credentials for an individual coach can be time-consuming and expensive. If a prospective coach does have some industry credentials, this can be a signal of his or her commitment to the craft. However, there are very good coaches who have not undertaken the credentialing process. In either case, you should ask if the coach has been trained in a certified coaching method.

Introduction/Alignment: I encourage you to meet with a coach on an introductory level. Are you comfortable with the rapport you two have? Are you confident that he or she is the right person to help you?

Exercise: Would You Benefit from Working with A Career Coach?

Our friend and contributor to this book, Mike Johnson, offers the following exercise to potential clients to help them identify if their job search could be enhanced by working with a Career Coach like himself.

Take a few minutes to honestly answer the following questions, then compare your answers with the key at the bottom of the page to help discover if career coaching is right for your search.

Quiz – Career Search/Career Development

I have completed a self-assessment/personal inventory.	Y/N
I have identified my key strengths, skills, and core competencies.	Y/N
I can positively communicate the reason I left my most recent employment.	Y/N
I have identified my key message/Personal "Brand," communicating my value.	Y/N
I have named my target occupations/job roles.	Y/N
I have validated my target market (organizations of interest that may be looking for my skills).	Y/N
I have completed an updated, targeted Resume and uploaded to selected job board sites.	Y/N
I have updated my online LinkedIn profile to reflect my message.	Y/N
I have created an Action Plan for my career search/advancement, using key disciplines.	Y/N
I have researched Industry & Company data for my target industry and organizations.	Y/N
I have a networking strategy and am intentionally reaching out and meeting new people.	Y/N
I have developed a target list of Recruiters and have contacted them.	Y/N
I am conducting informational meetings with key contacts in areas/organizations of interest.	Y/N
I know how to respond to behavioral-oriented interviewing questions.	Y/N
I keep a regular scorecard/checklist of my plan for personal accountability.	Y/N

Could a Coach help me in my career development?

If you responded "Yes" to ...

12-15 items:
You have developed a strong career transition, job search, or career advancement strategy. A Career Coach can help you in clarifying your goals and the impact of your message, in refining your plan, in uncovering and overcoming obstacles, and in keeping momentum toward your goals.

7-11 items:
You have some level of confidence and skills for successful career transition and job search. You may need some fine-tuning. Take a good look at statements where you answered "No." A Career Coach can help you consider how to turn these into "Yes" statements, and improve your effectiveness.

0-6 items:
Consider a Career Coach to discuss your strategy and how to incorporate disciplines and tools into your campaign. Although this may seem frustrating and time-consuming, today's job market demands new skills and approaches to clearly stand out from other candidates and to be successful.

Surviving Financially

lthough the stigma associated with being unemployed (or "in transition") is lessening as more and more people experience this unexpected bump in their careers through no fault of their own, there is one issue often plaguing job seekers that virtually all of them are afraid to talk about: finances.

Most people live to their income. By that, I mean that people tend to buy the most house they can afford, the best cars, and take vacations that are commensurate with their income. That is why you may have been making $50,000 a year and thought, "If I could just make $75,000, I'd be set," only to discover, upon earning that magic $75,000, you still don't have any extra money. We expand our lifestyle to our income. We all know we should be saving but we aren't very good at that. We'd rather spend it.

Bankrate.com is a popular website offering basic financial advice and a wide range of financial calculators. In January of 2017, Bankrate conducted a survey of 1,003 adults on the topic of the ability to meet emergencies financially. The bad news is that the survey discovered that 57% of Americans did not have enough cash available to cover an unexpected $500 expense. Incredibly, that is actually a 5% improvement from the same survey done in 2016.

Perhaps we like to think that an emergency will never happen to us. Maybe our brains would rather assume that we will always have a paycheck every other Friday. Unfortunately, that blind faith is not very helpful in the "real" world. About half of the respondents in the survey reported that they had, indeed, incurred such an unexpected expense in the previous twelve months.

So you are certainly not alone as you contemplate your finances while digesting the realization that your income has stopped and you have to find another job. And if you are in that majority of Americans who cannot afford to go very long without a paycheck, the pressure of finding something fast is likely weighing on you.

Your parents probably taught you that it isn't polite to discuss finances. Furthermore, you are probably uncomfortable telling others you are struggling financially. That could feel like a double whammy of failure. "Not only have I lost my job, I'm poor!" And while speaking with a financial advisor might be helpful, they aren't interested in helping you if you can't pay! (Frankly, they typically aren't trained in helping people in transition anyway).

This chapter is included to help you identify some self-help strategies to get through this time of unemployment. Not knowing how long it will last can make any planning difficult, to say the least. But there are techniques that might be available to you depending on your circumstances.

Unemployment Compensation

File for unemployment. Many people, due to pride or perhaps the feeling that their finances are sufficient to carry them for a while, either delay or completely avoid filing for unemployment compensation. My advice to you is, do it anyway.

Unemployment compensation is administered by each state, so each system is different, as well as the methods to file and receive benefits. Some commonalities include a requirement that you apply for jobs while you are drawing unemployment and that you have a need for the compensation. Because each state has different rules, I can't give you much specific direction on filing beyond telling you to contact your state unemployment office and get the process started.

In many states, the process takes some time. You may file the paperwork this week and not begin receiving benefits for several weeks or a month. The earlier you start the process, the earlier you will start getting benefits.

Most states also reduce your benefits by the amount of your other income. This sometimes has the opposite effect of the one desired, as job seekers will avoid part-time or temporary employment because their benefits will be reduced.

Beyond the additional income you may receive from your state unemployment compensation, once you have registered, you are most likely eligible to being accessing resources you can employ in your job search as well. The main goal of any effective unemployment office is to get you back to work (and off the public dole). They almost always offer job search classes such as resume building, interviewing practice, and even skills development such as Excel or PowerPoint.

It may be humbling to ask for help from your government. But if a tree fell on your house and caused $10,000 of damage, you would immediately call your insurance company and expect payment. That's what insurance is for! The same can be said for unemployment compensation. Whether you know it or not, your employer(s) and you have been paying into that system for your whole working life just in case this exact situation happened. Now it's time to collect on that "insurance" policy. There is no reason not to. (While companies may have to pay more unemployment taxes if they have particularly bad histories of claims, you will never be punished for claiming benefits.)

Health Insurance

Have you ever noticed that when you have something really important going on, you often catch a cold or the flu? That isn't coincidental! Stress in our lives reduces our defenses and weakens our immune systems. We are more likely to get sick when we are stressed. And what is more stressful than a job search?

When you left your last job, assuming your company had more than twenty employees, you were offered the option of continuing your health insurance policy that your company offered. This is often called COBRA, which refers to the Consolidated Omnibus Budget Reconciliation Act of 1974 (Now you understand why it is just called COBRA!). Under the COBRA law, a departing employee may elect to continue his or her current health insurance plan for up to eighteen months after termination. This is an option, not a requirement. However, most people simply make that election and continue with the plan they are comfortable with.

If you were fired, you are probably still eligible for COBRA coverage. The law states that only those terminated for gross misconduct do not have to be offered COBRA. In fact, even if you quit voluntarily, the company still must offer COBRA as an option.

If you decide to continue with COBRA, you may experience some sticker shock. Most companies subsidize the health coverage for their employees, meaning the company pays some of the premium and the employee pays some of the premium. When you elect COBRA coverage, the entire premium is then charged to you each month. So, in addition to your paycheck stopping, your health insurance costs may double or triple.

The good news is, there are some alternatives.

First, the Affordable Care Act, also known as the ACA and/or Obamacare, offers a range of health insurance plans through the online government marketplace (www.healthcare.gov). As of this book, there is some uncertainty as to potential future changes to the ACA, but it is still a viable and, to some, very attractive option.

Normally, healthcare under the ACA is only available during periods of open enrollment. However, there are several exceptions and losing your job and/or your current healthcare policy qualify as exceptions. So, before you accept the COBRA option blindly, log on to the health insurance marketplace and check your options.

In most cases, the policies available to you on the marketplace will not be as comprehensive as the one you had through your employer. If you do find some that match your employer's plan through COBRA, they may be quite pricey (Plans are "graded" like the Olympic medals; bronze plans are more basic, silver is better, gold plans are the best in terms of coverage offered). If you do locate a plan you like, you can do all the application paperwork right online.

If the COBRA plan is better, you might wonder why you should consider one on the government marketplace at all. The answer is cost. You will pay out of pocket regardless, so it is important that you choose a plan you can afford. If you can afford to maintain your current plan, great. But if money is tight, you may have to accept a less than ideal plan in exchange for a lower monthly cost.

Another option, which is often an excellent choice, is to join a spousal plan. Of course, this requires that you are married (or, in some states and many companies, a qualified domestic partner) and that your spouse or domestic partner has a job with a health plan. Like the ACA, your spouse's health plan will typically allow you to join as a dependent if you have lost your job and/or your previous insurance coverage. In general terms, it is usually much less expensive to add another person to an existing plan than it is to purchase a new stand-alone plan.

The other option is something new but gaining popularity very quickly. It is called religious health sharing plans.

The ACA has multiple requirements that, for insurance policies to qualify as ACA policies, they must cover such things as birth control. Some religious organizations object to that. So the ACA has a built in exception for religious health sharing organizations. In simple terms, it is generally accepted that a person who is part of a religious health sharing organization is exempt from the ACA requirement that everyone have health insurance (or pay a penalty – which you can probably ill afford right now).

Because religious health sharing organizations are exempt from the ACA, their plans do not have to follow the rules applicable to traditional health insurance plans. Primary among those is the requirement for birth control. But another important difference is that, while an ACA insurance company may not decline an applicant due to a pre-existing medical condition, a religious health sharing plan can reject those with pre-existing health issues. So if you do have a pre-existing condition, you may have to stick with COBRA or an ACA policy.

Because of that exception to ACA requirements, the plans offered by religious health insurance sharing organizations vary widely. Some have maximum benefit limits (such as $100,000 or $1,000,000) while others do not. Likewise, premiums differ. However, these plans are often much less expensive than traditional options such as COBRA and ACA policies.

Before terminating your current coverage or opting against COBRA, BE SURE YOU QUALIFY FOR OTHER COVERAGE. If you decide to use a religious health sharing plan, opt out of COBRA, then are declined for coverage, you can't change your decision and your only option may be an ACA policy. And you may not be eligible unless you are in the open enrollment period. Make sure you don't have a gap in coverage!

<u>Finding Assets</u>

If you are like most people, the thought of not having that regular paycheck is scary. That money is the source you have employed for years to pay all those bills coming in. Now the income has stopped but the bills have not. It is natural to begin thinking that you have no way to pay those bills. Fortunately, for many that isn't quite the case. You may have assets that, while you might prefer not to access them, if the need is great enough, can provide sources of short-term income.

Admittedly, everyone's situation is different. But the following are four different sources that you may have to help you survive the income drought.

Retirement Plans

You probably have what's called a defined contribution plan such as a 401k from your former employer (it may be something similar depending on the industry you are in). And in the haze of decisions you had to make when you left your last employer, you were probably offered the option of moving your retirement plan elsewhere or leaving it with your employer. When you have so many other stressful events foremost in your mind, worrying about something like that is probably pretty far down the list. So, like others, you probably just left it where it is.

While that is not a devastating decision, moving it is probably the better option. Here's why.

First, 401k plans (and the like) are subject to administrative requirements such as top-heavy testing, which result in higher related costs. Put more simply, it is more expensive to maintain a company plan than an individual one. And those costs have to come from somewhere and the only assets to use are yours (and others in the plan). So, the bottom line is, it is less expensive for you to maintain your own account than to leave it in your company's hands.

Second, an individual account allows you much easier and quicker access to the money should you need it. If you need a few thousand dollars to pay your bills from your 401k, you will most likely need to complete a form, send it in, and someone will have to determine if the request meets the definitions of a qualified distribution. This takes time and gives you an additional hoop or two to jump through. Having your own personal account avoids all of that. With your own account, you can request money for any reason and the request is processed immediately. Indeed, most of the time you can even do it all online.

So, of course, the question is, to what can you move your 401k or other plan? In most cases, you can move your "qualified" retirement plan account directly into an Individual Retirement Account and avoid it counting as a distribution, thus causing taxation and possible penalties. But there are enough differences between plans that you should consult with your tax professional to make sure.

You saved and saved for your retirement and will likely feel as if those assets are off limits. Honestly, they should be. Accessing your retirement savings should be a last resort. But if you have to pay bills, you have to pay bills. And if there are no other options, you may not have a choice. Your retirement plan may be the biggest liquid asset you have.

Here are two considerations as you decide whether to tap into your retirement. First, with a few exceptions, if you are under 59 ½ when you make a withdrawal, the IRS will assess a 10% penalty on the withdrawal. This is in addition to the normal income tax you will incur. So, for example, if you take a pre-59 ½ distribution from your IRA of $10,000, you will not only have taxable income of $10,000, but also a penalty of $1,000 on top of that. (Don't get scared by the word "penalty." You aren't going to jail because you took money from your IRA. It is simply a discouragement for people to raid their retirement accounts. Even though 10% is a lot of money, it is pretty much equal to the employment taxes that are taken from your paycheck anyway, which you won't pay on an IRA distribution).

Second, and more obvious, is the fact that you may be cannibalizing your retirement. Unfortunately, there are no ways around that. In the grand scheme of your retirement plan, taking a distribution here or there may not have a dramatic effect on your retirement itself. But if you are living off your retirement savings for a significant period of time, that's a different story.

You also need to check your state unemployment rules. Some states reduce your unemployment benefits if you are taking money from other investments.

Life Insurance

An often overlooked source of income is life insurance. Many people have policies that they have either not thought about or are simply unfamiliar with the rules regarding drawing income from them. This discussion is only relevant to cash value life insurance. Term insurance does not offer any income potential other than when the insured passes away.

Before you surrender all your life insurance policies, you should understand that the usual cardinal rule on life insurance is that you do not terminate an existing policy unless you absolutely no longer need the coverage. And you may have bought a policy years ago for a reason (like putting the kids through college if you die) and the reason is still valid. The reasoning behind avoiding such a surrender is two-fold. For one, life insurance policy premiums are calculated when you purchase it. The premiums are determined using your current age at purchase. As you get older, purchasing a new policy will be more expensive while the cost of your previously purchased policy will remain the same. If you terminate a life insurance policy with the plan to repurchase it later when your income is stable again, your premiums may be considerably higher. But, again, if you have to surrender it to live, you have to surrender it.

Second, not everyone can get life insurance. Life insurance is subject to underwriting, which is the process by which the insurance company looks at your health at the time of application and sets a premium based on that information. In the alternative, the company may decide that you are too great a health risk and decline to sell you the insurance at all. So, if you surrender the policy that you bought when you were in great health at age twenty-two, then have a heart attack, when you apply to get it back you will either pay a much higher premium (due to both age and poorer health) or be declined completely.

Assuming you have a cash value life policy and need to access that cash, surrendering it completely is not your only option. You likely have the choices of a partial surrender, leaving some of the insurance in effect, or taking a loan.

Partial surrenders. Life insurance policies can be complicated instruments with lots of moving parts. For example, if you have a whole life insurance policy, it virtually always pays dividends. Those dividends may be a relatively painless way to find some money.

Unless you have elected to have your annual dividends paid to you directly, or are using each dividend to pay less in premiums the following year, they are being collected in the policy in some form. Sometimes they are left "on deposit," which simply means that the insurance company has deposited your dividends in an interest bearing account, very similar to a savings account. Those dividends simply sit there year after year and earn interest, albeit not much in most cases. If you have a life insurance policy with dividends on deposit, you can simply request payment of any or all of the dividends and interest accumulated. The insurance company will mail you a check and, best of all, it will have no effect on your life insurance policy.

You may also have your dividends on an option called "paid up additions." This option is very popular and is most common in whole life insurance policies sold in the last twenty or twenty-five years. With paid up additions, each dividend is used to purchase more life insurance. This makes your policy increase in face value but also in death benefit. If you have had a whole life insurance policy for many years and the dividends purchasing paid up additions, you could see your death benefit amount double or even triple and your cash value accumulate accordingly.

If you do have a whole life policy with paid up additions as the dividend option, you may request that the paid-up additions be surrendered and the cash value of those paid up additions be paid to you. Exercising this option will drop your death benefit (all the way to the original amount if you surrender all of your paid-up additions) and your cash value will shrink as well. But the basic policy will still be intact. It will simply look and act like the original policy you purchased years ago.

There are other versions of cash value life insurance available such as universal life insurance and variable life insurance. These usually don't pay dividends but may still offer you options to remove money while still retaining the base policy. Check with your agent for your options.

Another option available on cash value policies of any kind is taking policy loans. A loan on a life insurance policy is exactly what it sounds like. You are "borrowing" the cash value. Most people have a hard time understanding why they have to borrow their own money, but with cash value life insurance, the insurance company actually still treats the money as if it is in the policy. So they still credit interest or pay dividends even though you are holding the money. Consequently, to offset this interest or dividend, the company charges an offsetting interest rate when you borrow.

The biggest benefit in borrowing against a life insurance policy is that the policy continues in effect. As long as you pay the interest on the loan each year, your policy will not be adversely affected. However, you can also borrow the interest each year. This is certainly an option, especially when money is tight, but be warned: if the loan plus the interest accumulates too high, the policy will terminate, and you will lose your insurance coverage.

Policy loans are often a great option because of the income tax treatment. If you surrender a policy (or part of a policy), you are typically income taxed on any policy gain (meaning the money you receive over the premiums you paid in). Not so with policy loans. Loans are not income taxable, even if you take more out than you have put in! There is one catch, though. If the policy does terminate because the loan and interest has accumulated, you will be taxed on the gain at that point. So try not to let it lapse.

If you get back on your feet and pay the loan (and interest) back, the policy goes on like nothing happened. If you die before the loan is paid back, the death benefit is reduced by the amount of the outstanding loan and interest. Your beneficiary still gets the rest.

Annuities

The popularity of annuities seems to come and go. When the stock market is on the way down, annuities with fixed interest rates or guaranteed minimum interest rates become popular. When the markets are going up, people would rather chase the higher potential gains and these fixed interest annuities are not nearly as popular. (There are variable and indexed annuities that allow you to earn stock market-like gains ... and losses. These tend to pick up the slack when fixed annuities are not popular).

I have seen TNG members who have annuities that they have forgotten about, or, perhaps, they thought they couldn't access the money. But often times, the money is accessible – with some rules.

Annuities are subject to very special and peculiar tax laws. First, deferred annuities (which are ones that earn interest over time instead of paying out immediately) come with an IRS penalty should you take any money from them before you turn age 59 ½. There are a few exceptions to this penalty such as death and disability, but you should talk to your tax advisor before assuming you qualify. The IRS penalty for an early withdrawal is 10% of the gain removed from the policy.

Second, whenever you remove money from your annuity, the IRS says that you are taking the gain out first. This means that withdrawals are always going to be income taxable as long as the balance of the annuity is more than what you have paid in.

<u>Home Equity Loans</u>

Although they should really be a last resort, I have seen situations in which a home equity line of credit (or HELOC) has helped a job searcher survive for a few months. The scary thing about taking money from a HELOC is that it creates another monthly expense. However, once again, if it is a matter of life or death, it may be the only option.

The trick with a HELOC is that you must have had it set up before you were unemployed. After all, banks do not like to loan money to people who don't have income to pay it back! But many banks are aggressive in offering HELOCs to their customers even if they don't have a need for them at the time. They can sit dormant and only be accessed if/when needed, like when you are unemployed!

I put this option out there with trepidation. Use it at your own peril.

Exercise:

For many people who are worried about their ability to survive without a steady paycheck, making a budget can result in some much needed comfort.

Using Excel or even a pen and paper, write down all of your monthly expenses. Eliminate the ones that you can live without. Then add a little in because you will need some additional cash for spending money, entertainment, and other things.

Compare your expected income including severance pay, your unemployment compensation, and any other sources of income. Then identify any shortfall.

If you do have a monthly shortfall, look at your other investments covered in this chapter and see if you can access those to make it through this period of unemployment.

STARTING A TEAM NETWORKING GROUP

If you are interested in replicating the success through The Team Networking Way, please contact the authors at our website:

TeamNetworkingWay.Com

THE JOB SEARCH FUNNEL

The effort and information you put into the top of the funnel is directly connected to the success you'll have at the bottom!

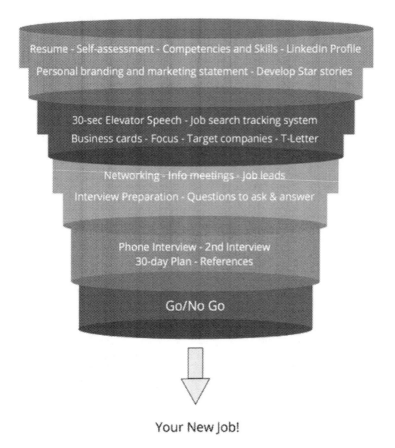

Resume - Self-assessment - Competencies and Skills - LinkedIn Profile

Personal branding and marketing statement - Develop Star stories

30-sec Elevator Speech - Job search tracking system

Business cards - Focus - Target companies - T-Letter

Networking - Info meetings - Job leads

Interview Preparation - Questions to ask & answer

Phone Interview - 2nd Interview
30-day Plan - References

Go/No Go

Your New Job!

RESOURCE LIST

1. Your local government Workforce Development office

    *   For example, in Indiana, this is through the WorkOne system

2. Your local Unemployment office

    *   They will have the tools and process for you to file for unemployment insurance, and reporting required

3. Your local church congregation

4. Outplacement services

    *   If you have been reduced in force, sometimes the company will secure an outplacement service on your behalf (such as Right Management, Lee, Hecht, Harrison and others). If you have this benefit, take full advantage of their resources and coaching.

5. A local Job Search Support group (such as Team Networking Group)

6. Job Boards

    *   Indeed.com, and 1-2 other niche job boards in your target industries/occupational areas

7. Recruiters active in your locale and target industries/occupational areas

   - Develop your working "short list"

8. Your Strategy: Your list of target organizations as potential employers

9. Networking Contact Sheet: Build from your network as you expand it into your target organizations

10. Key Tools

    - Your computer! Email, calendar management, word processing, spreadsheet
    - Jobscan.co – compares your resume against a target job description
    - Salary research (payscale.com, salary.com, etc.) – research market salary range for your target roles (both national and regional/local)

MARKETING PROFILE TEMPLATE

\<Name\>*

\<Current Job Title\>

\<Contact information, including LinkedIn profile\>

WHO I AM

\<brief narrative, e.g. 30-second introduction\>

WHAT I PROVIDE

\<key skills, capabilities, and personal attributes you bring to an employer, e.g. a condensed version of your Summary from your resume\>

WHAT I'VE DONE

\<key accomplishments, e.g. highlights from top 3 STAR stories\>

-
-
-

HOW I ADD VALUE

<ways that you can contribute to the new group's success>

-
-
-

TARGET ROLE(S)

<target jobs/areas of interest>

-
-
-

TARGET COMPANIES

<target areas/groups/divisions/companies>

-
-
-

DESIRED CONTACTS

<roles/name>

---

*a professional headshot in the upper righthand corner is optional

WORKING WITH RECRUITERS

Recruiters are an integral part of the job market "infrastructure." Recruiting is a necessary function of the hiring process, whether the person is working in a permanent role for the employer, or an independent agent. Recruiters generally "stay in their lane" – their niche or focus, as part of their mission or under their contract to an employer.

A common misperception is that recruiters are synonymous with "Headhunters." This is far from the truth. Most recruiters, in fact, fight this stigma. Many, if not most, independent recruiters are small businesses, small teams, or individuals. They are experts in networking. You should view a recruiter as a *new potential resource*. Acknowledge them as professionals and never, never turn down a request for a networking conversation with one. It benefits both of you – they get to know a bit about you, your strengths, and what you're looking for, and you have another person by your side in the job search.

The best types of recruiters juggle priorities, working on their client's behalf *and* on their candidate's behalf. At the end of the day, recruiters as advocates for both!

Types of Recruiters

Contract/Executive Recruiters (you pay): This business model is decreasing, but it does still exist in some areas. They charge you a fee, and some offer a guarantee of refunding some portion of the fee if you are not placed within a given timeframe.

Talent Acquisition Recruiters (employer pays): This is the predominant business model of the majority of recruiters. They work under contract to the employer, who pays them after a candidate is placed with the company.

Staffing agencies: They do recruiting for their client employers, but also manage staffing under contract (temporary, or temp-to-hire roles). Often the individual works for the agency (who pays them) and is placed at an end client location.

Value of Recruiters

- Access – to target employers, other employers you may not know about, other recruiters
- Network – a source of introductions for you
- Focus/Niche – many are serving a particular industry or professional discipline
- Awareness – of hidden job market (what may be in the works)
- Creativity – "marketable, place-able candidates" – they can act as an advisor to their clients
- Insight – of why you were not selected following an interview, for a company with whom the recruiter is working with you

Challenges & Strategies

Time management.

At any given time, a recruiter may be working with several employers, dozens of candidates, and maintain a network of hundreds of contacts. A recruiter may appear to be easily distracted and not on your timeline (because they *aren't* on your timeline). Keep in mind who their paying client is (generally the employer, not you).

They don't tend to follow up with you.

Be aware of a recruiter's caseload on a given week, and the number of employer clients that person is most likely serving. Recruiters give time to their priority clients and candidates (just as you would). If a specific recruiter isn't responsive or tends to be very short-sighted on only a specific posting, don't put them on your short list!

Multiple recruiters can be working for the same employer & job posting.

If you see a job posting from a job board, you should do two things. 1) Check with a recruiter on your "short list" to see if they can work with you – let them help you. Mention your search strategy to the recruiters you are working with – most will follow a "first in/ first out" practice and defer to another recruiter if they were working with you first.

2) If the recruiter cannot help, apply directly to the employer's web site (vs. via a job board). Be aware that exposures may exist or develop for you to be working with competing recruiters. Be prepared to make the hard choice and disengage if necessary.

Strategies

- Develop a short list, know those recruiters by name
  - Active in your target industry, locale, and/or professional discipline
  - When you can, seek to meet the local recruiter in person

- Be proactive - keep regular contact with your short list (Don't expect the recruiter to be proactive on your behalf)
- Follow up promptly on all requests for information
- Keep a positive attitude – if certain recruiters have a pattern of not following up with you, drop them from you short list!

- Don't forget that as a job seeker, you can get discouraged and frustrated – and recruiters can be an easy target! Don't take your frustration out on them.

Success factors

Maintain your online presence: Prepare a professional LinkedIn account, with contact information visible. Be aware of your online presence (Google yourself). Add Facebook and Twitter accounts for job search if desired. Over 90% of recruiters actively research potential candidates on LinkedIn.

Network! Above all else, recruiters are active networkers. They circulate.

- o *Be visible:* attend forums, conferences, seminars, civic group gatherings.
- o *Give out your business card* (with resume on the back) freely.
- o *Be well-rounded:* Volunteer with trade organizations as well as local charity or community outreach groups.
- o *Say YES to all invitations:* even if not interested. This is an opportunity to gather useful information and meet people of influence.

Contact recruiting firms proactively in your field. Know the recruiter's business model (who is paying).

Act in good faith: Recruiters will ask and need to know your salary expectations, benefit package content, ability to relocate, restrictions, etc. There should be no surprises.

Summary

Recruiters can be part of your network of key resources aligned with your career goals! They are a key part of your strategy, so don't ignore them. Instead, find a few that resonate with you and cultivate them.

STAR STORIES

S.T.A.R. Stories are short narrative examples of
- a **S**ituation or **T**ask you were presented with,
- the **A**ction you took to navigate the situation, and
- the **R**esult.

The logic is that how you behaved in the past will predict how you will behave in the future. You demonstrate how you helped provide value before as an illustration of how you can provide value to a new employer, department, or division.

Suggestions:
- Identify 6-8 examples from your past experience where you demonstrated top behaviors and skills that employers typically seek. Think in terms of examples that will exploit your top strengths / "selling points."
- Some of your examples should be totally positive, such as accomplishments or meeting goals.
- Also include situations that started out negatively but either ended positively or you made the best of the outcome.
- Vary your examples; don't take them all from just one area of your life. Use examples from your most recent work experience, but also internships, class projects, activities, team participation, or community service.
- Review any performance evaluations, key project reviews, etc. for key accomplishments for which you were acknowledged, or are most proud of.

- Wherever possible, quantify your results. Did you:
    - o Reduce costs, increase revenues/profits? Impact bottom-line? (How?)
    - o Meet/exceed company objectives? (In what way?)
    - o Identify, create or implement a new procedure or system? (Results?)
    - o Identify or solve a major problem for your department or division? (Results?)
    - o Develop or do something for the first time at your company? (Results?)
    - o Improve employee performance or productivity? (How?)
    - o Receive any special recognition or awards? (Why? What was the business impact? What actions
    - o produced that result?)

Example (Advertising)

Situation / Task (ST): Advertising revenue was falling off for my college newspaper, and large numbers of long-term advertisers were not renewing contracts.

Action (A): I designed a new promotional packet to go with the rate sheet and compared the benefits of circulation with other ad media in the area. I also set up a special training session for the school of business professor who discussed competitive selling strategies.

Result (R): We signed contracts with 15 former advertisers for daily ads and five for special supplements. We increased our new advertisers by 20 percent year-to-year.

<u>**Epilogue:**</u> List key skills you used in the Action that you took.

STAR Story   Name:

SITUATION / TASK

ACTION

RESULT

SKILLS

Marketing Yourself – Personal Branding Worksheet

Key Strengths

-
-
-
-
-

Key Traits, Characteristics / Key Words

-
-
-
-
-

Key Skills

Transferable:

-
-
-
-
-

Knowledge-based/Industry or Domain-specific:

-
-
-
-
-

Core Competencies (TOP Skill areas from above)
(What do you love to do so well, that you cannot imagine, NOT doing?)
-
-
-

Target Roles/Focus
-
-
-

Printed in the United States
By Bookmasters